LIFE
WRITING

Literary/Cultural Theory provides concise and lucid introductions to a range of key concepts and theorists in contemporary literary and cultural theory. Original and contemporary in presentation, and eschewing jargon, each book in the series presents students of humanities and social sciences exhaustive overviews of theories and theorists, while also introducing them to the mechanics of reading literary/cultural texts using critical tools. Each book also carries glossaries of key terms and ideas, and pointers for further reading and research. Written by scholar-teachers who have taught critical theory for years, and vetted by some of the foremost experts in the field, the series Literary/Cultural Theory is indispensable to students and teachers.

Series Editors

Allen Hibbard
Middle Tennessee State University

Andrew Slade
University of Dayton

Herman Rapaport
Wake Forest University

Imre Szeman
University of Alberta

Krishna Sen
University of Calcutta

Scott Slovic
University of Idaho

Sumit Chakrabarti
Presidency University, Kolkata

Also in the series

Psychoanalytic Theory and Criticism	**Queer Studies**
Postcolonialism Now	**Marxist Literary and Cultural Theory**
Feminisms	**Frantz Fanon**
Jacques Lacan	**Mikhail Bakhtin**
Dalit Literature and Criticism	**Deconstruction and Poststructuralism**
Ecocriticism	
Postsecular Theory	**Edward Said**
Nations and Nationalisms	**Diaspora Theory and Transnationalism**
Periyar	
Popular Culture	**Subaltern Studies**

LITERARY/CULTURAL THEORY

LIFE WRITING

A SHORT INTRODUCTION

RAJESH V. NAIR

Mahatma Gandhi University, Kerala

Orient BlackSwan

LIFE WRITING: A SHORT INTRODUCTION

ORIENT BLACKSWAN PRIVATE LIMITED

Registered Office
3-6-752 Himayatnagar, Hyderabad 500 029, Telangana, India
Email: centraloffice@orientblackswan.com

Other Offices
Bengaluru, Chennai, Guwahati, Hyderabad, Kolkata, Mumbai, New Delhi, Noida, Patna

© Orient Blackswan Private Limited 2024
First published 2024

ISBN 978 93 5442 431 1

Typeset in Aldine 401 BT 10.5/13 *by*
Akhil Offset Printers
Hyderabad 500 020

039319

Printed at
Shree Maitrey Printech Pvt. Ltd., Noida

Published by
Orient Blackswan Private Limited
3-6-752, Himayatnagar,
Hyderabad 500 029, Telangana, India
Email: info@orientblackswan.com

The publisher has endeavoured to ensure that the URLs for external websites referred to in this book are correct and active at the time of going to press. However, the publisher has no responsibility for the websites and can make no guarantee that a site will remain live or that the content is or will remain appropriate.

Contents

Acknowledgements

At the outset, I should admit that the entire journey of writing such an introductory book on life writing was a huge learning experience. I could learn a lot, but at the same time, I could also unlearn certain things. Of course, my specialisation in Life Writing Studies gave me the courage and confidence to embark on this project. The bourgeoning interest of readers in this field and the dire need for a concise and easy-to-read introductory book on life writing inspired me to complete this project successfully.

My sincere gratitude goes out to the following people, whose help, inspiration, and direction have been invaluable in the writing of this book:

I take this opportunity to thank Sreenath S., Managing Editor, Humanities at Orient BlackSwan for placing trust in me. I hope I have met his expectations.

I would like to thank Krishnan Unni P., K. Narayana Chandran, and Pramod K. Nayar for their inspiration and ongoing support.

My father, late G. Vasudevan Nair and my mother, Radhamani P. N. have been very supportive through their unwavering love and support. My wife Aswathy and kids Abhijeet, Gowrie and Nirmal have shown exemplary understanding and patience throughout this arduous journey.

The anonymous reviewer of the manuscript has helped me immensely with sharp comments and queries. I must place on record that it was an academically enriching experience.

I am grateful to Aditi Jha for her editorial expertise, sharp attention to detail and valid suggestions to enhance the quality of the book.

My colleagues at School of Letters, Mahatma Gandhi University, Kerala have been very supportive, and their warmth has always helped me to be more 'adventurous' in my academic pursuits. I highly appreciate their camaraderie and friendship.

I thank my friends, researchers, and other students for their affection and positive vibes – G. S. Jayasree, Parvathy Das, Priya K. Jose, Sabitha S. Babu, Lakshmi C. M., Rajasree, T. G. Harikumar, Reenu S. John, Ponnu Liz, Chaithanya Antony and Geethu Nandakumar.

To the readers of this book, I would like to extend my deep appreciation for showing interest. I sincerely hope and wish that my work will benefit and enlighten the academic community in general.

Chapter One

Introducing Life Writing

TERMINOLOGY

Life writing is an umbrella term that alludes to the innate human urge to share one's experiences and emotions with the outside world. Indeed, though autobiography is the most common form of life writing, several subgenres articulate identities, including biography, memoir, diary, journal, letters, emails and biopics. According to various critics, self-narration is referred to by a variety of labels, including 'life writing', 'life histories', 'life tales', 'life narratives', 'auto/biographies' and 'life texts'. Their core preoccupation is self-articulation whether by the subjects or by others. However, we may keep in mind that these terms are used flexibly and rather interchangeably among scholars, with no consensus on a single term.

Life writing broadly encompasses visual, oral and even digital narratives, and it is useful to take this approach since it allows for an investigation of how distinct identities are inscribed across multiple modalities and their ideological contexts. Indeed, while writing/telling about lives is sometimes considered an offshoot of the protagonists' excessive individualism, one must disregard the therapeutic influence of such narratives on authors, and in some circumstances readers, after the documentation of poignant experiences. Additionally, we can view such live texts as inspiring stories which give readers vignettes of survival. Recently, the academic world across disciplines has taken a serious interest in Life Writing Studies from a variety of perspectives: literary, historical, psychological, sociological, anthropological, political, medical, linguistic and ecological, to name a few. Today, there are academic journals such as *Biography: An Interdisciplinary Quarterly, Life Writing, European Journal of Life Writing* and *Auto/biography Studies* exclusively devoted to this field of study. There are also institutions, such as the Oxford Centre for Life Writing and the University of Hawaii's Centre for Biographical Research, that provide possibilities for serious research in this field. There are thousands of books and articles being written about life writing, and many places host seminars, conferences and writing workshops for people interested in this field.

THE SELF AND BODY

The 'self' is a nebulous concept that refers broadly to the inner sentiments and psychological experiences that are intimately connected to one's identity. Indeed, the experiential dimension of self is what determines one's self-awareness and uniqueness. We may be aware of the multiple manifestations in which we can perceive self in totality – phenomenological self, linguistic self, material self, ideological self and self as desire – as Norman Denzin brilliantly puts it in *Interpretive Biography*. If the phenomenological self is all about one's thoughts, perceptions and ideas about oneself, the linguistic self is the textualised 'I' that becomes a part of narrative discourse. The self can also be materialised in the form of autobiographies or biographies, which are available in book form. In the case of the ideological self, every individual is considered to be constituted by one ideological block or another and self-as-desire points out that the 'subject always returns to desire and its meanings in his or her life' (Denzin 31–32). However, the self is defined from a variety of perspectives, including philosophy, psychology, linguistics, postmodernism and neuroscience. Early debates on self, particularly during the enlightenment period, focused on unified and autonomous selfhood. Nevertheless, by the second half of the twentieth century, with the rise of postmodernism and the unique contributions of figures such as Freud, Nietzsche, Joyce, Proust, Derrida and Lyotard, the self was being perceived as divided, fragmentary and multiple. Indeed, postmodern theories have emphasised the textuality of the self, as a floating signifier constructed by language. The self has also been decentred by Derrida's deconstructive approach. So, during the postmodern era, the traditional definition of autobiography as a text that shows a cohesive and unified self changed, and the autobiographical self started to be heavily questioned.

From the traditional school of thought's cohesive, self-reflective autobiographical 'I', we can now perceive the existence of multiple 'I's in a life narrative, replete with gaps and silences. As previously mentioned, language plays a vital part in the development of the self, as the latter is no longer taken for granted as it used to be earlier. 'The patterns and meaning of a "life" are not found or given, but made. They are "inscribed"' (Jolly, Volume 2, 801). However, the inscription of self has profound ideological underpinnings. Olshen makes an interesting distinction between the autobiographer's self and the autobiographical self: 'They are not at all the same. The one "belongs" to the living person, the experiencing subject; the other is bound in text, a textual signifier, the autobiographical ego, or "I". This figure may be called the persona' (801).

According to Sidonie Smith and Julia Watson, autobiographical subjectivity has many different aspects and is shaped by things like memory, experience, identity, embodiment and agency. An autobiography is a retrospective account of our past experiences written in the present tense. These memories are also affected by our sense experiences, especially when we choose some important events from the past. The notion of auto/biography involves the insistence that accounts of other lives influence how we see and understand our own and that our understanding of our own lives will impact how we interpret other lives (L. Stanley i). Memories are inextricably linked to their surroundings; when we recall significant events from the past in order to construct a life story, we invariably include certain social events in which certain individuals were involved. As a result, life texts provide several interpretations of a specific era. Whether they may be considered alternative histories is another matter altogether. However, subjects' identities, notably their class, caste, religion and race, are cultural markers that ultimately transform life writing into cultural texts. The life writer who selects instances of self-inscription will, in all probability, be choosing just those occurrences that they deem important to mention. It is thus evident that the process of recalling memories involves politics as life writers either support or challenge cultural norms concerning the formation of a body and an identity; bodies become sites where knowledge and new ideas are generated.

Historically, due to societal restrictions and the fear of scandal, women have been hesitant in their writing of sexual exploits, for fear of objectification and over-sexualisation. Men, too, have not been open about their sexuality in their life histories. It is only recently that a paradigm shift in this moral censorship has occurred – women are now telling their stories of rape and bodily violence; men are debunking 'masculinity' myths; marginalised sexual groups are speaking out against heteronormativity; transgender people are proudly reclaiming their sexual identity; and those who are differently abled write about their social stigma.

In Life Writing Studies, bodies become texts or signifiers that inscribe/embody multiple subjectivities through different genres and sub-genres. In trauma life stories, the body represents dissent and resistance. Postcolonial life narratives inscribe postcolonial bodies in the context of colonialism's aftermath and the formation of a new nation state. Gendered bodies are negotiated in various life narratives; autobiography is the prominent form that is used to document female subjectivity; subjects belonging to other sexualities, including transgender people, also often adopt the autobiographical mode for reinscribing their bodies. Disability life writings write about physically-disabled and, more importantly, socially-disabled bodies resulting from social stigma. Autopathographies narrate diseased bodies. Illness narratives document painful bodies. The representation of the body in cyberspace offers new possibilities for life writing research, especially in the aspect of voyeurism and sexuality. Profile pictures and automediacy through uploaded videos in archives such as YouTube expands the dimensions of subjectivity and bodily inscription. Life writings in the form of books commodify bodies and offer them as material artefact for circulation and consumption. Statues and memorials are material manifestations of the bodies of subjects. The notion of selfhood is intricately linked to the physical body, as the narrative of an individual's body unfolds from infancy to adulthood, ultimately culminating in death. Throughout this journey, many forms of written accounts, such as biographies and autobiographies, emerge to assess and assign particular value judgements to the life experiences of the subject.

FORMS OF LIFE WRITING

Interviews, conversations, well-known ballads, as-told-to narratives, folk narratives passed down through anecdotes and even institutional records, like those for a prison or the military, have all been used as forms of life writing with overlapping and contradictory narrative strategies and presentational techniques. In fact, this genre is separated into several branches, each of which suggests a particular subject stance, including autobiography, biography, journal, memoir and diary. As we may already know, the story of a person's own life experiences, values, dreams, recollections and fears is defined as an autobiography. It might be viewed as a journey of self-discovery for both the eager writer and the observant reader. However, in the late eighteenth century, it gradually started to be recognised as a distinct literary genre and catalysed intense discussions on important issues like authorship, selfhood, representation and the line separating fact from fiction (Nair 2).

PARALLEL LIVES

Plutarch, the Greek writer, is known as the father of biography. His is known primarily for *Parallel Lives*, a collection of biographies of orators, soldiers, legislators and statesmen of ancient Rome and Greece. In writing *Parallel Lives*, Plutarch followed the comparative method for each biography, comparing one Roman with a Greek; the famous one being the comparison between Greek orator Demosthenes and the Roman orator Cicero. His tone is didactic and moralistic, and he used many interesting anecdotes in the twenty-six short biographies. Each biography begins with the birth, adulthood, successes and ends with the death of the hero. In 1579, Sir Thomas North published the famous English translation *Lives of the Noble Grecians and Romans*,

SHORT TAKES

and later John Dryden and Izaak Walton also published English translations of the work.

Diaries, journals, memoirs, letters and recollections are all examples of autobiographies. These forms of writing are so ubiquitous that Paul John Eakin considers it 'not only a literary text but much more: a daily identity practice, and even an expression of the rhythms of consciousness' (90). He identifies three motives behind our irresistible urge for self-presentation: 'We are trained to do it as children, we use it to explore our deepest existential questions, and it just may confer an adaptive value for the organisms that we are. I conclude by suggesting my sense of autobiography's place in the larger scheme of things: life writing as cosmogram' (90). He continues: 'I do so, nonetheless, to suggest that the autobiographical act is in its way also an act of alignment, a mapping of self and its place in the world, and a personal building program to articulate the shape of a life' (103–04).

SHORT TAKES

THE PASTON LETTERS

The Paston Letters is a unique collection of family correspondence of letters between the Paston family of Norfolk, their staff and friends from fifteenth century to seventeenth century, spanning the medieval, Tudor and Stuart periods. The collection is a rich source to understand the political and social history of England. The letters throw light upon the daily life and troubles of an ambitious family based in England. From the philologist's point of view, the letters are a valuable source of the evolution of the English language. A collection of more than 1000 items, *Paston Letters* include the correspondences of members such as William, John I, John II and John III in the form of legal records, local and national news, gossip, etc. Four volumes of *Original Letters* (1787–89) were edited by one John Fenn of East Dereham whereas a fifth volume was completed by William Frere. Later, James Gairdner re-edited *The Paston Letters 1422-1509* in six volumes in 1904.

A diary is a type of autobiography that is frequently written in the form of a book and is structured daily, documenting events that take place throughout a day or a certain period. Diaries are commonly maintained for long term and in most cases, are solely meant for private circulation. A memoir is a fragmented narrative covering only a portion of one's life; typically, a memoirist focuses on public issues rather than personal experiences. In contrast, a diary is a record of an individual's intellectual and spiritual development, a method of self-discovery and self-satisfaction. These social documents acquire newfound significance because the individuals who created them attempted to supply their version of 'reality'.

A paradigm shift has taken place towards the disadvantaged and subaltern parts of society, such as racial minorities, homosexuals and Dalits, as a result of the memoirs and biographies of the 'great and famous'. This modern movement in life writing has gathered strong proponents from the fields of history, anthropology and feminist studies, among other academic subfields. The use of silence is one of the strategies, if not the primary method, that life historians employ in order to protect themselves from the cultural dangers that are present in autobiographies, biographies, legends and even diaries. John Dryden is credited with having first used the term 'biography' in 1683, in the prologue to his translation of Plutarch. The term 'biography' comes from the medieval Greek word *biographia* – *bio* means 'life' and *graphein* means 'write'. Thus, the term means 'writing about lives'. A subject's biography is more than just a recounting of objective facts such as birth, education, occupation and death; rather, it sheds light on how a subject views these events, thus allowing for the study and interpretation of that subject's personality. The primary premise of the biographical technique, which is that one's life may be recorded and portrayed in a book, is currently up for debate (Nair 3–4).

EMINENT VICTORIANS

Eminent Victorians (1918) is a collection of four biographies – Cardinal Henry Edward Manning, Florence Nightingale, Dr Thomas Arnold, and General Charles Gordon – written by Lytton Strachey. The author has revolutionised the biographical genre by writing a biography which attacks the revered figured figures of Victorian period through Freudian psychoanalysis

SHORT TAKES

rather than celebrating them. In fact, the text shattered the notions of Victorian moral supremacy – Cardinal Manning is portrayed as a manipulator within the church, Florence Nightingale as disagreeable, Arnold's rigidity of educational model is discussed, as well as Gordon's tactlessness and ferocity of temper. Though *Eminent Victorians* brought forth a new approach in conceiving lives, that is debunking of subjects, Strachey has been accused of being prejudiced and sometimes careless in not seriously investigating the original sources.

SCOPE OF LIFE WRITING

Interdisciplinarity is the cornerstone of Life Writing Studies, and we can see how it intersects with a range of disciplines such as sociology, philosophy, anthropology, linguistics, science and human rights, among others, providing it with a great deal of diversity, scope and dimension. The following section unequivocally corroborates it.

With the advancement of science, life writings about scientists became popular – particularly after World War II – in the form of autobiographies, biographies, letters, diaries and journals. However, it is worth noting that such literature from the male-dominated Western culture is favoured over that from the East. Paul de Kruif's *Microbe Hunters* (1926) is a classic example of popular scientific biography. Among notable examples are physicist Richard Feynman's *Surely You're Joking, Mr. Feynman!* (1985), James Watson's *The Double Helix* (1968), Florence Nightingale's *Letters and Reflections*, Basil Miller's biography *Florence Nightingale: The Lady with the Lamp* (1947) and Marie Curie's biography of her husband, *Pierre Curie* (1963). Apart from this, there is a genre known as scientific autobiography, which includes popular books by Fritjof Capra (*The Turning Point*, 1982; *The Tao of Physics*, 1976) and Oliver Sacks' literary works such as *Awakenings* (1973) and *A Leg to Stand On* (1984).

Life writing has grown in prominence as a technique of sociological study, particularly where concerns about identity and narrative configurations are at stake. Human agency is central to sociological research, and this sociological life narrative method was popularised in the 1970s by the French sociologist Daniel Bertaux.

Autobiographies are increasingly being used to investigate national identity, class, gender and social mobility. Carolyn Steedman examined prevalent views about class and gender identity through the lens of her family stories. Apart from the letter collection *The Polish Peasant in Europe and America*, the sociological value of diaries and letters has also been popularised by French theorists Philippe Lejeune, Roger Chartier and others.

Migrant life writing has developed into a multidisciplinary field of study, addressing cross-cultural issues of cultural identity, home and belonging. Numerous non-fiction forms, including autobiographies, memoirs, letters, biographies and diaries, are used to convey diasporic experiences. *Night Train to Mother* (1989) by Ronit Lentin, Alex Haley's *Roots: The Saga of an American Family* (1977), *Water with Berries* (1971) by George Lamming and Salman Rushdie's *The Satanic Verses* (1988) are all excellent examples. Diasporic writing is like autoethnographic writing in that the author makes connections between personal experiences and the culture of their origin.

Psychological life writing allows readers to peer into people's inner worlds, aspirations and fears. Psychobiography, a hybrid form combining psychology and biography, is a popular kind of life writing that rather than recounting a subject's whole life, concentrates on crucial events. Erik Erikson's *Gandhi's Truth* (1969) and *Young Man Luther* (1958), as well as Gordon Allport's *Letters from Jenny* (1965) are good examples of psychobiography. In addition to Dan McAdams, Silvan Tomkins, Rae Carlson, Ted Sarbin and Jerome Bruner, there are other notable writers in the realm of psychological life writing.

The link between philosophy and life writing is, to put it mildly, complicated, and a variety of genres, such as autobiography, biography, memoir, diary, disability narratives and essays, all express philosophical observations about life. Additionally, there are high-quality autobiographies of philosophers with a literary bent, such as George Santayana's *Persons and Places* (1944–53), Bertrand Russell's *Autobiography* (1967–69) and Rousseau's *Confessions* (1782–89). Besides this, there are biographies of philosophers, including Isaiah Berlin's *Karl Marx: His Life and Environment* (1939), Peter Brown's *Augustine of Hippo* (1967), E.C. Mossner's *The Life of David Hume*

(1954), James Miller's *The Passion of Michel Foucault* (1993) and Ray Monk's *Ludwig Wittgenstein: The Duty of Genius* (1990) and *Bertrand Russell: The Spirit of Solitude* (1996). It is possible to see that these many genres of life writing redefine the self on a philosophical level.

LIFE OF SAMUEL JOHNSON

James Boswell's biography *Life of Samuel Johnson* (1791) is considered one of the finest biographies written in English language. Boswell's biggest advantage was his close association with his subject for almost 21 years which helped the former rely more on the authentic sources in the form of journals, interviews and letters. The biography was so well-written and set such a standard that in Thomas Macaulay's opinion it eclipsed the actual subject himself. Boswell explains Johnson's wit with interesting conversation and anecdotes. Though Boswell appreciates Johnson's writing skill, wit and precision, he does not shy away from describing the idiosyncrasies of his subject.

Life writing has a close connection with anthropology because of the innate, human urge to tell lives. In fact, according to Hornung, 'the anthropological turn of life writing, is related to the emergence of the human subject from the medieval social order of the "chain of being" into a more autonomous existence' (qtd. in Jolly, Volume 1, 38). Individualism was celebrated in early Renaissance humanism, as seen in the writings of Thomas More, Martin Luther and Montaigne, among others. Gradually, we can observe the emergence of cultural anthropology as a field and the growing interest in the study of the human race. Numerous autobiographical writings in nineteenth-century America, such as Ralph Waldo Emerson's *Representative Men* (1850), Henry David Thoreau's *Walden* (1854) and Walt Whitman's *Leaves of the Grass* (1855) were manifestos of extreme individualism. Frederick Douglass and Harriet Jacobs' African–American slave narratives focused on anthropology and race. Later, Sigmund Freud's psychoanalytic theory introduced an entirely new concept of the self. Claude Lévi-Strauss' contribution to structural anthropology in the twentieth century helped to advance the field, and his portrayal of indigenous people in works such as *Tristes Tropiques* (1955), an autobiographical account of field trips to the Brazilian Indians in the Amazon region (1935–39), is noteworthy.

According to Ivan Crozier 'sexuality is employed as a portal into the "real" life of the person – a secret self, rather than that conveyed by the public deeds and achievements of the person' (qtd. in Jolly, Volume 1, 805). Along with class, religion and other factors, it plays a critical role in the construction of one's identity. Certain biographies place a premium on sexuality, particularly under the influence of Lytton Strachey, author of *Elizabeth and Essex* (1928). Autofiction, a subgenre of autobiography, fictionalises a person's life, and certain works, such as Marcel Proust's *Remembrance of Things Past*, place an emphasis on sexuality. Additionally, there are memoirs, autobiographies and testimonials by homosexuals and transgender individuals that examine the nature of sexuality and its significance in the development of individual identity.

Nature is narrated via several forms of life writing, such as autobiography, biography and personal essays. *The Voyage of the Beagle* (1839), Alfred Russel Wallace's *The Malay Archipelago* (1869), Mary Kingsley's *Travels in West Africa* (1897), Jane Goodall's *In the Shadow of Man* (1971) and *Through a Window* (1990) and Dian Fossey's *Gorillas in the Mist* (1983) all portray different facets of nature.

There has been a surge of interest in the link between pedagogy and life writing, particularly in educational research, that emphasises the personal experiences of students and instructors. Jerome Bruner's (1984) cognitive science studies and the social constructivism paradigm have bolstered the life history approach in education.

With the pervasiveness of trauma around the world in the form of genocide, slavery, colonialism, sexual abuse, pandemic, etc., one can find a convergence between trauma and life writing. However, the dimension of trauma widens from private to public or personal to historical; 'trauma is never exclusively personal; it always exists within complicated histories, both individual and collective. Placing a personal history of trauma within a collective history compels one to consider that cultural memory, like personal memory, may also possess "recovered" or "repressed" memories' (Jolly, Volume 1, 886). Indeed, traumatic life experiences serve as counter-histories by exposing not only the physical wounds caused by particular violent acts but also the mental/psychic scars, thereby fighting all manner of human rights abuses and oppressive power structures in their hydra-headed manifestations. How to express severe suffering in language is a significant issue, and while language may prove woefully insufficient, writing heals both the victim and the community as a whole. Trauma memoir is the most common type of life writing in this field, and we have some moving texts such as Gregory Williams' *Life on the Color Line: The True Story of a White Boy Who Discovered He Was Black* (1995), Jean Dominique Bauby's *The Diving Bell and the Butterfly* (1997) and Kathryn Harrison's *The Kiss* (1997). Other important works on the subject of trauma and life writing include Art Spiegelman's *Maus: A Survivor's Tale* (1986), Nancy Venable Raine's *After Silence: Rape and My Journey Back* (1998), Lauren Slater's *Prozac Diary* (1998) and Caroline Knapp's *Drinking: A Love Story* (1996).

The dysfunctional body and its relationship to identity construction may have contributed to the growth of life stories about illness and disease near the end of the twentieth century. According to Kay Cook (Jolly, Volume 1, 456), illness life narrative 'encompasses narratives of mental illness, especially schizophrenia and bipolar disorders; heart disease; neurological and neuromuscular disorders, such as stroke and multiple sclerosis; and addiction to alcohol and other drugs, to name a few' (456).

However, illness life writings have led to a sense of pessimism and anxiety, since they often culminate in ageing and death. Alternatively, they act as a foil for medical jargon. Several of these stories operate as conversion narratives as well, since they highlight how specific themes inspire readers via their survival and conversion stories. With the Holocaust and other atrocities against human rights occurring around the world, autobiographies and memoirs have dominated the literature on disease. G. Thomas Couser coined the term 'autopathography' to describe disease-life narratives. May Sarton's *After the Stroke* (1988), William Styron's *Darkness Visible: A Memoir of Madness* (1990), Audre Lorde's *The Cancer Journals* (1980, and *Burst of Life*, 1988), Nancy Mairs' *Plaintext* (1986) and Juliet

Wittman's *Breast Cancer Journal: A Century of Petals* (1993) are just a few examples of life-texts that address illness.

The positionality of the autobiographical self has become one of the major concerns in literary studies with the popularity of postcolonial, gender and cultural studies approaches (Wagner-Egelhaaf 413). 'In fact, the autobiographical self moves on the border between the past and the present; therefore, autobiographical texts will always enable conclusions pertaining to the time of their composition' (413). At the beginning of their book *Life Writing and Space*, Eveline Kilian and Hope Wolf underscore the significance of space in identity construction: 'Who we are, and how we narrate ourselves, depends on our ability, our desire or failure, to locate our identities within space and concerning certain places. Formation of the self often relies on spatial movement, on (re)locating the self in different places and social spaces' (1). In life writing, the physical journey runs in parallel with the 'inner, metaphorical journey of the self' (1). However, traditionally, temporality was a major concern in the narrative where events are organised in a linear sequence and thinkers such as Paul Ricoeur have stressed the 'configuration' (22) of narrative structure.

The enlightenment legacy of the linearity of individual development and the subsequent social progress (Kilian and Wolf 2) was later questioned by thinkers including Robert Tally Jr when he preferred a 'spatial turn' instead: 'Critical theorists, historians, philosophers, and geographers certainly would now hesitate to proclaim much faith in the universal progress of history in the wake of such destruction, and a changing view of temporal movement may have opened the way to those who demanded that greater attention be paid to spatial concerns' (12). Frédéric Regard opines: 'when it comes to self writing, the question is not so much "who am I?" as "where am I?"' (16).

The spatial turn is in conjunction with historical and technological developments, and in some cases, we witness displacement being reflected in fragmented narratives. No wonder, in the context of Palestinian writing, Edward Said comments: 'Our characteristic mode ... is not narrative, in which scenes take place *seriatim*, but rather broken narratives, fragmentary compositions, and self-consciously staged testimonials, in which the narrative voice keeps stumbling over itself, its obligations, and its limitations' (38). Feminist thinkers such as Doreen Massey argue that the place/space binary is unwarranted and, like space, the place is also '"unfixed, contested and multiple" as well as "open and porous"' (5). According to Michel de Certeau, place and space have a dynamic relationship, and the place is 'brought to life and appropriated by the individual through spatial practices: *"space is a practiced place"*' (qtd. in Kilian and Wolf 4). Mobility is the crucial factor, and the street, which is systematically demarcated by urban planning, is turned into space by the walkers. Thus, 'movement decentres places, just as it decentres selves and their place-related identities. Hence, mobility initiates a dynamic of (re)creation and decreation of the self…' (qtd. in Kilian and Wolf 3). People who refuse to be tied down to a location by crossing over and connecting through frequent mobility change the social and political dynamics associated with that location.

Literature can produce 'alternative spaces' (qtd. in Kilian and Wolf 5) and 'narratives of the self modulate the interrelation between physical and mental spaces and constitute a kind of "heterotopia"' (Foucault) in which alternative configurations of social spatiality and individual subjects' engagements with spatial parameters can be experimented with (qtd. in Kilian and Wolf 5). 'The autobiographical subject becomes the centre of enunciation and organises the world around that centre, an operation that bestows a certain degree of spatio-political agency which is first and foremost textual, and therefore subject to the laws of language' (5). Regard (16) addresses the 'poetic spacing of the self', that is, the autobiographical subject undergoes not only geographical displacement but also dislocation in language and discursive formation. Taking a post-structuralist angle, we can see that the subject is a wanderer who is always in motion and is never rooted in a place.

POLITICS OF LIFE WRITING

Edward Bruner says, in analysing the process of life writing, that there are clear, inevitable gaps and silences between reality, experience, and expression created by the impact of ideology (7). He observes: 'A life lived is what actually happens. A life experienced consists of the images, feelings, sentiments, desires, thoughts, and meanings known to the person whose life it is…. A life as told, a life history, is a narrative, influenced by the cultural conventions of telling, by the audience, and by the social context' (7). Ideology motivates people from all socioeconomic backgrounds to write autobiographies and biographies, as well as to inscribe their versions of subjectivity in the works they make. According to Denzin (32), these ways of writing and the things that go along with them force, call, and create different visions of real people as subjects.

Life writing has been become extremely politicised as people from all walks of life have gained the ability to express themselves and inscribe their subjectivities. However, there may be a shift in the focus of this kind of writing, with life texts now being produced about individuals from society's so-called subaltern or marginalised portions, as well as those from the highest social strata. Both autobiographies and biographies are constructed around 'epiphanies' in the subject's life (Denzin 22). Although many people believe that life writings are objective, factual and 'truth-like', it is important to understand that facts can be altered by the storyteller to further his/ her hidden aim. Rather than pursuing genuine people, it is more important to comprehend how texts and other forms of speech shape individuals. Denzin divides life into two levels: surface and deep. A person is characterised on the surface level by what he or she does in daily life, which includes routines and behaviours; on the deeper level, a person is defined by a feeling, moral, sacred, or inner self. Indeed, the cultural politics of life writing can be studied on several different levels, including class, caste, nation, race and gender, to mention a few.

REFERENCES

Bruner, Edward M., editor. 'The Opening up of Anthropology.' *Text, Play, and Story*. The American Ethnological Society, 1984.

Denzin, Norman K. *Interpretive Biography*. Sage Publications, 1989.

Eakin, Paul John. *Writing Life Writing Narrative, History, Autobiography.* Routledge, 2020.

Foucault, Michel. "Of other spaces" [1967 and 1984]. *Diacritics: A Review of Contemporary Criticism*, translated by J. Miskowiec, vol. 16, no. 1, 1986, pp. 22–27.

Jolly, Margaretta, editor. *Encyclopedia of Life Writing: Autobiographical and Biographical Forms Volume 1.* Fitzroy Dearborn Publishers, 2001.

---. *Encyclopedia of Life Writing: Autobiographical and Biographical Forms Volume 2.* Fitzroy Dearborn Publishers, 2001.

Kilian, Eveline and Hope Wolf. *Life Writing and Space.* Routledge, 2016.

Massey, Doreen. *Space, Place and Gender.* Polity, 1994.

Nair, Rajesh. V. *Politics of Life Writing: A Study of Mahatma Gandhi's Select English Biographies.* Zorba Books, 2016.

Regard, Frédéric. "Topologies of the Self: Space and Life-writing." *Mapping the Self: Space, Identity, Discourse in British Auto/Biography.* Publications de l'Université de Saint-Étienne, 2003, pp. 15–30.

Ricoeur, Paul. "Life in quest of narrative." *On Paul Ricoeur: Narrative and Interpretation*, edited by D. Wood. Routledge, 1991, pp. 20–33.

Said, Edward. W. and J. Mohr. *After the Last Sky: Palestinian Lives.* Columbia UP, 1999.

Stanley, L. "Introduction: Lives and Works and Auto/Biographical Occasions." *Auto/biography*, vol. 3, nos. 1 and 2, 1994, pp. i–ii.

Tally Jr., Robert. *Spatiality.* Routledge, 2013.

Wagner-Egelhaaf, Martina, editor. *Handbook of Autobiography/Autofiction.* De Gruyter, 2017.

Chapter Two

Life Writing: Early Phase

LIFE WRITING IN ANTIQUITY

At the beginning of the fifth century BC, Ion of Chios wrote short biographical sketches of the lives of both Pericles and Sophocles. Cornelius Nepos, a historian who lived in the first century BC, was the author of the life of Pomponius Atticus, a Roman art patron. Later on, the disciples of Socrates and Jesus Christ were told to write about their teachers. Plato's *Life of Socrates* is another great example, along with *Apology* and *Phaedo*. After that, we come across figures like Plutarch, Suetonius and Tacitus, who are all considered professional biographers. The growth of Christianity led directly to the writing of St Augustine's autobiography, *Confessions.*

The history of biography can be traced back to remote antiquity. The engravings in old caves that reflect diverse events, such as a successful hunt, could be regarded as the first forms of biography. The ancient Egyptians built pyramids, which became symbols of their inflated egos and need to make up stories about their triumphs and deeds. The writing system used to record such victories was cuneiform, which was chiselled into stone or clay tablets (Nair 10–11). The ancient Greeks looked at man as a part of society, not as something separate from it. This led to biographies which were disjointed, short and not of great quality. The earliest texts still in existence are Xenophon's *Memorabilia* (a collection of Socrates' dialogues), Isocrates' *Life of Evagoras* and Theophrastus' *Characters*. All three of these were written in ancient Greece around the fourth century BC. The Romans were known for writing condensed, rhetorical and argumentative biographies of famous people. People often refer to Plutarch as the father of biography because he was the one who penned *Parallel Lives*. During the Roman Empire, when emperors with totalitarian powers ruled the country, biographical writing and historical writing traditions began to mix. During the early Middle Ages in Europe, which lasted from 400 to 1450 AD, the Roman Catholic Church was both the most powerful political group and the only repository for historical knowledge and documents. The first modern biographers were monks, hermits and priests. They mostly wrote about holy people like popes, martyrs and saints. These 'instructive' biographies were written to enlighten and moralise the common man. *The Life of Charlemagne*, which was written in the ninth century by Einhard, Charlemagne's courtier, is an important example of the only biography from this period that fits into that mould. *Le Morte d' Arthur* (1485) by Thomas Malory is a good illustration of the popularity of biographies of kings, knights and tyrants during the late Middle Ages. People wrote in their own languages because of the Renaissance and influence of contemporary humanist ideas. This resulted in the development of a new type of biography known as secular biography. This genre focused on non-religious figures, such as painters and poets. *Lives of the Artistes*, written by Giorgia Vasari in 1550, is an example of such a groundbreaking biography.

LIFE WRITING IN THE MIDDLE AGES

The lives of saints, as written by the priests of the time, was a prominent literary genre during the Middle Ages. Notable works in the field of biography include Eadmer's *Life of Anselm*, Bede's *Ecclesiastical History of the English People* of the eighth century and Einhard's *The Life of Charlemagne*. Bishops and abbots commissioned the majority of medieval biographies for a variety of reasons. These biographies were written about men and women involved in religious vocations throughout that period (Winstead 7). Monasteries used life histories to promote their status, attract new members and indoctrinate the general public by teaching them certain morals and beliefs based on their religion. In addition, the papacy validated the contributions of specific subjects' lives through the documentation of their lives, which allowed at least some of those subjects to be approved for canonisation. Although we may recall that Latin was the language used to write such life stories, it is essential to remember that some of the biographies were also translated into English. The medieval English biographers emphasised the facts and correctness of their work, and they exerted a great deal of effort to carry out interviews, cross-check data, and other similar activities. As a result, each subject or saint was required to extol particular redeeming virtues.

The biographies written on administrators, politicians, recluses and other types of people typically presented their subjects in an idealised light. Most of them were written in prose, with only a few in verse. The virtues that were valued in these lives were studiousness, scholarship, humility, persistence, patience, compassion, charity and tolerance, apart from moderation (19). The private lives of its subjects, including the specifics of their friends, co-workers and family members, were given a greater amount of attention in the early medieval biographies that were written. Garnier of Pont-Sainte-Maxence's *Life of Thomas Becket*, written around 1175, adhered to factual data while incorporating a literary approach, creating a form of romance for the work's readers. As has already been said, early biographies had parts that were like autobiographies. Augustine's *Confessions* and Guibert's *Monodies* are two great examples that help prove this point.

In the sphere of medieval life writing in Europe, we can discern a pattern, that is, the life writings about continental women, visionary nuns, urban anchoresses, beguines of the Low Countries, tertiaries of southern Europe, and many more (46). In fact, in contrast to the situation in England, there were biographical descriptions of notable holy women such as Elizabeth of Hungary, Catherine of Siena, or Bridget of Sweden. However, biographies of holy women dealing with Anglo-Saxon abbesses and legendary early Church heroines appeared in England during the late medieval period. These lives focused on women who lived during the early years of the Christian church (46). A short while later, we come across the unusual lives of Eve of Wilton (who lived around 1125 and died around that time),

Christina of Markyate (who lived after 1155 and died after that) and Margery Kempe (d. after 1438).

When we investigate the history of medieval life writing, one of the subgenres of medieval biography that needs to be analysed is the genre of medieval biographies of kings. Bede's *Ecclesiastical History*, William of Malmesbury's *Deeds of the English Kings* (1125), John Lydgate's *Fall of Princes* (circa 1439), Asser's *Life of King Alfred the Great* (circa 893), the anonymous *Life of King Edward* who rests at Westminster (1065–07) and Aelred of Rievaulx's *Life of Saint Edward* (1163), all feature kings as prominent figures. There were also works like *The Deeds of Stephen* (1148–55) and *The Deeds of Henry the Fifth* (1416–17), which focused on sociopolitical events rather than the lives and accomplishments of the people being written about. These works were written in England. After some time had passed, John Blacman's *Compilation of the Meekness and Good Life of King Henry VI* emerged as a prominent example of a biography written during the medieval period.

Bede's *Life of Caedmon* and *Deeds of the English Bishops* (circa 1125), as well as a biography on Bede written by his admirer William of Malmesbury, are significant contributions to this field of study and were written during a period when literary biography flourished. *The Book of the Illustrious Henries* is a collection of biographies by Capgrave that focuses on the lives of famous Latin authors such as Henry of Ghent and Henry of Urmaria (c. 1446). During the time that he was waiting to be executed for treason, the theologian and philosopher Boethius composed his autobiographical book, *Consolation of Philosophy*, published around 524. Additionally, *Morte d'Arthur* (1469–70) written by Thomas Malory, *The Prologue to the Canterbury Tales* written by Geoffrey Chaucer, and the *Legend of Good Women* are all examples of works that contain autobiographical impulses.

The hagiographical tradition flourished in fifteenth-century England, as evidenced by works such as John Lydgate's *The Lives of Saints Edmund and Fremund* (1436) and *The Life of Saints Alban and Amphibalus* (1439), Alexander Barclay's *Life of Saint George* (1515) and Henry Bradshaw's *Life of Saint Werburga* (1521). Additionally, family letters and papers of the Pastons, Celys, Stonors provide 'sagas of birth, marriage, and death over several generations, so that a network of relationships, social circumstances, and contexts conveys to the modern reader a sense, perhaps illusory, of direct contact with the life of the time' (Davenport 130).

RENAISSANCE LIFE WRITING

Before the fourteenth century, there were lifeless panegyrics written about Italian monarchs by court humanists such as Simonetta. The Renaissance breathed new life into the form of biography, giving it a new lease on life as a literary genre. The works of Thomas More and John Colet, both of whom were active in the sixteenth century, are sometimes regarded as the beginnings of the genre of biography. Some of the earliest works of biography include Sir Walter Raleigh's *History of the World* (1614), Sir Thomas More's *History of Richard III*, Sir Fulke Greville's work on Sir Philip Sidney and Francis Bacon's *The Histories of the Raigne of King Henry the Seventh* (1622) and Sir Fulke Greville's work on Sir Philip Sidney.

When investigating the influence of British Renaissance life works, we may need to investigate the 'intellectual, theological, and technological' contexts (Mascuch 132). Because of the Renaissance, both the English and vernacular versions or translations of the Bible and other great classical works were made available to readers. Some examples of this include the English renditions of the Christian Bible, William Tyndale's New Testament and the Authorised Version of 1611. The Bible's influence resulted in the development of several biblical genres, including the epistle and prophecy, as well as a variety of personal letters and testimonials. John Foxe's *Acts and Monuments* (1563) and Miles Coverdale's *Certain Letters* (1564), as well as the pamphlets written by the early Quakers and other radical sectarians in the 1640s and 1650s are good examples of this type of writing.

In addition to these works, the monumental writings of humanist scholars such as Plutarch's *Parallel Lives*, which was translated into English by Thomas North in 1579, Tacitus' *The Life of Agricola*, which was translated by Henry Savile (along with Tacitus' *Histories*, 1591) and Suetonius' *The History of Twelve Caesars, Emperors of Rome*, which Philemon Holland translated in 1606, are noteworthy (Mascuch 133). Also noteworthy are Thomas More's *The History of King Richard the Third* (written c. 1513, printed 1557), George Cavendish's *The Negotiations of Thomas Wolsey, the Great Cardinal of England, Containing His Life and Death* (written c. 1556, printed 1641), William Roper's *The Mirror of Virtue in Worldly Greatness*, or, *The Life of Sir Thomas More, Knight* (written c. 1557, printed "Paris", 1626), the anonymous *History of That Most Eminent Statesman*, Sir John Perrot (written c. 1600, printed 1728) and Fulke Greville's *Life of the Renowned Sir Philip Sidney* (written c. 1610, printed 1652).

Classical life writing introduced the idea of living a good life to the British Renaissance, and works were written about men and women who lived up to 'the Renaissance ideal of being a human paragon' (133). The printed versions of funeral sermons, which depicted the saints' final hours and included biographical comments, were increasingly popular. Some of these works include Philip Stubbes's life of his wife Katherine, *A Chrystal Glass for Christian Women* (1591), William Hinde's *A Faithful Remonstrance of the Holy Life* and *Happy Death of John Bruen* (1625–27), and Edmund Staunton's *Sermon on Mistress Elizabeth Wilkinson* (1628). The historicity of these religious biographies is perhaps the quality that stands out the most to readers (133). Another popular type with readers were the last words spoken by convicted criminals before their execution. For instance, the numerous works produced by one author, Henry Goodcole, garnered a large readership. Another subgenre of British Renaissance life writing emerged around the same time that handwriting became more fashionable in the late sixteenth century and the early seventeenth century. This subgenre was made up of spiritual diaries written by famous people like Richard Rogers and Samuel Ward and by women from the upper class like Margaret Hoby, Grace Mildmay and Anne Clifford. The Renaissance's influence was felt in other genres as well, such as letters (written by Foxe, Coverdale and Katherine Paston), as well as the works of Henry Cecil, Henry Percy, Walter Raleigh and Christopher Guise, among others.

SEVENTEENTH- AND EIGHTEENTH-CENTURY LIFE WRITING

In early seventeenth-century England, we find a form called 'characters', popularised by Theophrastes, a disciple of Aristotle. However, during the early decades of the eighteenth century, women such as Lady Fanshawe, Lucy Hutchinson and Margaret Cavendish wrote biographies. In fact, Izaak Walton, a professor and biographer rose to prominence during this time period. Walton is known for penning biographical sketches of notable figures such as John Donne (1640), George Herbert (1670), the diplomat Sir Henry Wotton (1651) and ecclesiastics Richard Hooker (1665) and Robert Sanderson (1678). The eighteenth century ended with the publication of James Boswell's *Life of Samuel Johnson LL.D.*, (1791) an unrivalled masterpiece in biographical literature. Dr Samuel Johnson's book, *The Lives of the English Poets*, is credited with making him the father of biographical criticism. According to him, it is the responsibility of a biographer to convey the truth and reproduce a living character; the character does not have to come from a wealthy family in order for this to be accomplished.

A deeper understanding of the self was promoted by the philosophical and religious climate of the seventeenth century, and scholars like Rene Descartes engaged in significant debate on the concept of 'I'. One can notice a rise in the prevalence of and emphasis placed on narratives of personal experience (Snider 135). Despite the fact that the scientific temperament encouraged rigorous observation and attention to minute details of a subject, there was rarely any noticeable improvement in storytelling during the century (135). Character writing was based on stereotypical patterns – John Bunyan's popular spiritual autobiography, *Grace Abounding to the Chief of Sinners* (1666), defied true self-revelation, and the ecclesiastical narratives by Izaak Walton on notable English churchmen (John Donne, Sir Henry Wotton, Richard Hooker, George Herbert and Robert Sanderson) privileged 'exemplarity and instruction' (135) over truth. One of the most notable aspects of British life writing from the seventeenth century is the profound familiarity that existed between the biographers and the people they wrote about. This tendency is demonstrated beyond a reasonable doubt by Lucy Hutchinson's biography of her husband John (written between 1670 and 1675), as well as by Margaret Cavendish's account of her husband, the first Duke of Newcastle (1667). According to the theory put forth by Donald Stauffer in 1930, the terms 'biography' and 'biographer' did not come into use until the seventeenth century. The intellectual biography of the poet John Milton was written in 1694 by his nephew, Edward Phillips. The same biographer also compiled *Theatrum Poetarum* (1675), the first biographical guide to English poetry. This guide included brief sketches of some women writers, such as the Countess of Pembroke, Mary Wroth, Katherine Philips and Aphra Behn. Most of the autobiographies were not published during the lives of the subjects, and we can see a 'secular turn' in genres such as travel writing and memoirs. Some works, including John Fox's *Journal* (1694), depicted the century in detail.

The eighteenth century saw a more nuanced reflection of the self in British Renaissance life writing, yet 'tensions are typical in 18th-century auto/biography, where the endeavour to portray a cohesive voice is often undone by the instabilities of the "self" under development' (Quinn 136). In 1690, John Locke's *Essay Concerning Human Understanding*, a notable work that looked deeply into personal identity, was released. Another seminal work was Samuel Johnson's *Lives of the English Poets* (1779–81). However, James Boswell's *Life of Samuel Johnson* (1791) 'provides indications of private weakness amid records of public ebullience' (136), suggesting 'the Enlightenment's greater problem in maintaining its drive toward narrative perfection' (136).

A distinguishing feature of eighteenth-century life writing in England was its undeniable relationship with the novel, a relatively new genre at the time. Three of the many eighteenth-century books that claim auto/biography status are Daniel Defoe's *The Life and Adventures of Robinson Crusoe* (1719), Henry Fielding's *The History of Tom Jones, a Foundling* (1749) and Laurence Sterne's *The Life and Opinions of Tristram Shandy, Gentleman* (1759–67) (Quinn 136). Rousseau's *Confessions* (1781–89), William Godwin's *Memoirs* (1798) of Mary Wollstonecraft, Wordsworth's epic poem 'The Prelude',

Coleridge's *Biographia Literaria* (1817) and William Cowper's *Memoirs* (1816) enriched Romantic auto/biography.

During the eighteenth century, letters and diaries became popular, representing both the private and public spheres of a person. Letters from the Earl of Chesterfield to his son, letters from Samuel Johnson, letters from Burney to her sister, and diaries from Pepys are all relevant in this regard.

The autobiographical impulse was very strong in British Romanticism – it was defined by 'preoccupation with the self and its textualization' (Jones 139), and 'the artist had to assert his or her subjectivity as central to the writing itself' (139). Dorothy Wordsworth's *Alfoxden* (1798) and *Grasmere* (1800–03), Mary Wollstonecraft's *Letters Written During a Short Residence in Sweden, Norway, and Denmark* (1796), Mary Shelley's *History of a Six Weeks' Tour* (1817) and Ann Radcliffe's *A Journey Made in the Summer of 1794* all contributed to British Romantic life writing.

LIFE WRITING IN THE VICTORIAN AGE

James Parton, a professional biographer, was one of the first famous people to write about their lives in the 1800s. He published biographies of people like Aaron Burr and Andrew Jackson. Later, in France, works such as Benjamin Constant's *Adolphe* (1816) were published, which were autobiographies disguised as novels. Some major auto/biographies, such as Thomas Moore's *Letters and Journals of Lord Byron* (1830), Elizabeth Gaskell's *Life of Charlotte Bronte* (1857), James Froude's two volumes on Carlyle and John Forster's *Life of Charles Dickens* (1872–74) were published in nineteenth-century England. It should be noted that practically all of these works were hagiographic in nature.

Biography in nineteenth-century England was primarily concerned with 'public events and achievements in the public domain, autobiography with intimate experience' (Cockshut 142). In fact, there were categories such as success stories like Thomas Babington Macaulay's, William Gladstone's narrative on John Morley and Samuel Smiles' *Lives of the Engineers* (1861–62), stories about flawed heroes like Robert Burns (1828) and Walter Scott (1837–38), Robert Southey's *Life of Nelson* (1813) and humorous biographies like Thomas Hogg's *Life of Percy Bysshe Shelley* (1858). However, biographers refrained from exposing sensitive details, including sexual and financial matters of the public figures because of the obsession with Victorian morality (142).

Diary-keeping became a very popular practice in nineteenth-century England and appeared in published or manuscript forms. The main reasons for this were an increase in literacy, an increase in readership, the popularity of lending libraries, and so on. Both men and women as well as children assiduously followed diary writing, and bound books were used for the purpose. On the margins, spaces were left to jot down accounts and record anniversaries (Cook 143). Travel journals written by public figures and literary figures drew a sizable audience. Queen Victoria was a prolific writer; she wrote *Leaves from a Journal* (1855) and *Leaves from the Journal of Our Life in the Highlands* (1848–61). Literary figures such as Lord Byron, Mary Shelley, George Eliot, Gerard Manley Hopkins, Thomas Babington Macaulay and Walter Scott also wrote journals during the century.

Letter writing was also widely practiced in nineteenth-century England, and there was 'a ready market for published collections of letters, offering readers the illusion of intimacy with their authors, of entering their private lives while understanding more fully their public ones' (Onslow 144). Charles Lamb's volumes of letters, suffused with gossip and revelations and edited by his friend Sir Thomas Noon Talfourd, became very popular. This genre was a favourite among women too, and it allowed them to connect with public institutions like schools, universities and the gentlemen's clubs. Correspondence through letters helped people like Harriet Martineau, Elizabeth Barrett Browning and Mary Mitford establish social relationships.

REFERENCES

Cockshut, A.O.J. "Britain: 19th-Century Auto/biography." *Encyclopedia of Life Writing: Autobiographical and Biographical Forms Volume 1*, edited by Margaretta Jolly. Fitzroy Dearborn Publishers, 2001.

Cook, Kay. "Britain: 19ᵗʰ-Century Diaries." *Encyclopedia of Life Writing: Autobiographical and Biographical Forms Volume 1*, edited by Margaretta Jolly. Fitzroy Dearborn Publishers, 2001.

Davenport, Tony. "Britain: Medieval Life Writing." *Encyclopedia of Life Writing: Autobiographical and Biographical Forms Volume 1*, edited by Margaretta Jolly. Fitzroy Dearborn Publishers, 2001.

Jones, Angela D. "Britain: Romanticism and Life Writing." *Encyclopedia of Life Writing: Autobiographical and Biographical Forms Volume 1*, edited by Margaretta Jolly. Fitzroy Dearborn Publishers, 2001.

Mascuch, Michael. "Britain Renaissance Life Writing." *Encyclopedia of Life Writing: Autobiographical and Biographical Forms Volume 1*, edited by Margaretta Jolly. Fitzroy Dearborn Publishers, 2001.

Nair, Rajesh. V. *Politics of Life Writing: A Study of Mahatma Gandhi's Select English Biographies*. Zorba Books, 2016.

Onslow, Barbara. "Britain: 19th-Century Letters." *Encyclopedia of Life Writing: Autobiographical and Biographical Forms Volume 1*, edited by Margaretta Jolly. Fitzroy Dearborn Publishers, 2001.

Quinn, Vincent. "Britain: Restoration and 18ᵗʰ-Century Auto/biography." *Encyclopedia of Life Writing Autobiographical and Biographical Forms Volume 1*, edited by Margaretta Jolly. Fitzroy Dearborn Publishers, 2001.

Snider, Alvin. "Britain: 17th-Century Life Writing." *Encyclopedia of Life Writing Autobiographical and Biographical Forms Volume 1*, edited by Margaretta Jolly. Fitzroy Dearborn Publishers, 2001.

Winstead, Karen A. *Oxford History of Life-Writing: The Middle Ages*. Oxford UP, 2018.

Chapter Three

Life Writing: Modern Era

EARLY PHASE

Doris Lessing, one of twentieth century's most notable fiction writers, has made significant contributions to the genre of autobiography and biography with her works *Under My Skin* (1949), *Walking in the Shade* (1962) and *Alfred and Family* (2008). *Alfred and Family* is a mix of fiction and autobiography about her parents' lives. We see a shift in focus in the sphere of biography in the modern age, from biography as a powerful source of moral instruction to biography as a work of art. Virginia Woolf, Harold Nicolson, André Maurois and Lytton Strachey were key theorists during this transformation. Biographies became a big part of the publishing industry in the twentieth century, and their popularity has continued ever since. We see strong crossovers between history and fiction in new/modern biographies; this includes ironic detachment, literary modernism, deconstruction and historical reconsideration as new currents. During this time, biographical literature, like other forms of writing, went through a period of experimentation because of several reasons, such as breakthroughs in psychology, the influence of science and fiction. Sigmund Freud's effect was profound and far-reaching, paving the way for a new sort of biography known as psychobiography. Unexplored and taboo areas were investigated, giving innovative and never-before-seen details about a person's life. Live exemplifications include Erik Erikson's *Young Man Luther* (1958), *Gandhi's Truth: On the Origins of Militant Nonviolence* (1969) and Ernest Jones' *Life and Work of Sigmund Freud* (1955–57). Lytton Strachey's *The Eminent Victorians* (1918) marked the beginning of what Virginia Woolf referred to as 'new biography'. This form of biography, also known as the 'debunking' school, showed prominent leaders as charlatans and slaves to bogus values. The basic goal of an iconoclastic/debunking biography is to subvert the subject through numerous narrations. Psychological methods such as behaviour symbol analysis, interpretation based on the Oedipus complex, Jungian archetypal patterns of behaviour, and so on, have resulted in the psychobiography subgenre of biography.

Bringing the two realms of psychology and biography together, psychobiography gained popularity in the field of life writing. Subjects including Adolf Hitler, Sylvia Plath, Vincent van Gogh, William Shakespeare, Saddam Hussein, Richard Nixon, etc., have been studied by biographers, where a study of their inner lives and psychological development is undertaken. Apart from psychologists, anthropologists, political scientists and even sociologists contributed to this branch of life writing. Psychobiography has contributed to the study of many historical figures, including Mahatma Gandhi. Erik Erikson's *Gandhi's Truth, On the Origins of Militant Nonviolence* (1969), deals with a crisis in Gandhi's mature years.

In her 1927 essay 'The New Biography', Virginia Woolf offered a new approach to biography as a form. A biographer, according to her, has the freedom to combine reality and imagination, 'granite-like solidity' and 'rainbow-like intangibility'. In *Orlando: A Biography* (1928), Woolf attempted to mock and satirise the clichés of the form of biography by introducing a young nobleman who after living for three centuries is suddenly discovered to be a woman.

By the time the modern age set in, women had started taking a keen interest in recording their lives, and we have writers such as Sylvia Plath, Maya Angelou and Janet Frame as fine examples. Maya Angelou wrote a six-volume autobiography, starting with *I Know Why the Caged Bird Sings* (1970), through which she explores the racial segregation she encountered with her grandmother. Family memoirs proliferated in the second half of the twentieth century, and Joseph Randolph Ackerley's *My Father and Me* (1968) is a moving example. Truman Capote popularised the new form 'non-fiction novel' through *In Cold Blood* (1966). A loose and flexible genre, it portrays real historical figures and events while using the storytelling techniques of fiction.

HOLOCAUST LIFE NARRATIVES

The Holocaust has turned out to be a compelling site for inscribing trauma through a variety of genres of life writing, such as diaries, memoirs, autobiographies, biographies, testimonies and autobiographical fiction. Multiple forms of life writing have documented the excruciating pain and sufferings of victims and survivors and exposed to the world the atrocities and unthinkable plight of the Nazi pogrom of the Final Solution, which exterminated millions of Jews. These life narratives represent dehumanised subjectivities, and we may consider such narratives acts of survival and resistance – 'None of these plot lines bears any possibilities for satisfying resolutions; there is neither an open-ended journey nor poetic justice. Even survivor stories betray our expectations of heroism, suspense, the resolve of the human spirit, and triumph over adversity' (Lassner 185). According to Lassner, 'the act of writing the Holocaust can be cathartic and healing' (186), and we can see that authors find the act an emotional outlet, a way to vent their traumatic experiences. However, we can see the affective impact of life narratives on other survivors and readers; those victims who remained silent and unspeakable after the heinous atrocities around them find the writings on the Holocaust a healing experience, and readers find survivors' stories extremely motivating. However, Lassner identifies another angle, i.e., 'unyielding wrath' (186), in such life writings because they are essentially stories of resistance and protest against the crushing power structures. On the other hand, they prick the conscience of the self-indulgent who are in the comfort zone of their security. As one can see, 'an unconventional mixture of genres, incorporating both history and artistry, frequently makes works 'hard to classify', as they 'supplement an oral tradition on the verge of extinction', younger artists, writers, and filmmakers reflect on how to write it, a reflection on representation itself (Hartman qtd. in Lassner 185).

Language

The survival life stories of the Holocaust are characterised by 'conceptual, lexical, and social constraints combine with the complications of memory – traumatized, fragmented, interrupted, uncomprehending, and culturally shaped' (Lassner 182). This is due to language's inability to represent the unspeakable traumatic wounds caused by the disturbing experience. 'Lips try to speak but the mouth is paralyzed. A mouth cannot form words when it is dry, with no saliva' (Delbo 70 qtd. in Lassner 183). The 'gaps' and 'silences' in the narratives result from a traumatised self scarred by painful memories.

The diary is a popular literary form used for depicting the atrocities of the Holocaust. The writers of these diaries gave eyewitness accounts of important public events, but many of them, unfortunately, did not survive the Holocaust. In that sense, the diary as a genre cannot be regarded as a record of the private experiences of a diarist but instead a public document. For instance, Emanuel Ringelblum initiated the *Oneg Shabbat* Archive in 1939, 'a group effort to keep individual diaries that would record daily occurrences for documentation and testimonial purposes' (Lassner 180–81). Another project is Alan Adelson and Robert Lapides' remarkable collection, *Lodz Ghetto: Inside a Community Under Siege* (1989). *The Diary of a Young Girl* (1947) and Moshe [Moses] Flinker's *Young Moshe's Diary: The Spiritual Torment of a Jewish Boy in Nazi Europe* (1965) are the two works that made the diary a popular and poignant genre. However, the diary may be approached as a 'transgressive genre' (Wagner-Egelhaaf 547), as it 'transgresses the borders between body and text, since the "real" author and the narrator seem to fall into one in the diary. It transgresses the borders between public and private, marking the diary as a gendered genre since in the patriarchal paradigm the private counts as the realm of the female' (547). Another problematic issue is the question of agency and authenticity as in the form of diary 'borders between fact and fiction are transgressed because the "I" of the diary is subjective and unreliable with respect to the events it relates to; and, if one looks at writers' diaries, who often are avid diary writers, diaries often are artfully constructed' (547).

Another major branch of Holocaust life writing is the testimony, a form that 'combines the idea of recording a historical truth with testifying to its veracity as if a witness in court' (Jolly 438). One can see that these narratives were written with the 'intention of informing and reminding the post-Holocaust world about the atrocities committed; they usually concern the experiences of camp survivors' (438). Lawrence Langer's *Holocaust Testimonies: The Ruins of Memory* (1991) is 'a groundbreaking analysis of this genre, arguing that such testimonies reveal the "ruin" of memory and of lives in the aftermath of genocide' (438). Elie Wiesel's *And the World Was Silent* (1956), Primo Levi's *If This is a Man* (1947) and Wladyslaw Szpilman's *The Pianist: The Extraordinary Story of One Man's Survival in Warsaw 1939–45* (translated in 1999) are good examples of Holocaust testimonies which appeal to the conscience of the world.

Autobiographical fiction, another interesting genre of Holocaust life writing, is published as fiction but is based on the real experiences of a writer (438). Ida Fink's *A Scrap of Time and Other Stories* and Louis Begley's novel *Wartime Lies* (1991) are good examples. Commenting on the peculiarities of this genre, Lassner makes the following observation:

> In its many permutations, from the creation of a fictional first- or third-person narrator to imagined incidents and conflated or transformed time sequences, characters, and relationships, autobiographical fiction of Holocaust experience reflects attempts to find or construct coherence around those missing pieces or to try to make sense of the Nazis' deceptive and disorienting death machinery. (188)

Biography also forms a category of Holocaust life writing where biographers recount the experiences of their subjects who survived the Holocaust. Myriam Anissimov's biography of Primo Levi (*Primo Levi: Tragedy of an Optimist*, 1998), Art Spiegelman's two-volume account of his father's experiences during the Holocaust, *Maus: A Survivor's Tale* (1986 and 1991), are powerful narratives that inscribe traumatic experiences. Holocaust memoirs are potent narratives that capture the unthinkable atrocities of the pogrom. Fanya Gottesfeld Heller wrote the memoir, *Strange and Unexpected Love*, after her husband's death. Charlotte Delbo, a French political prisoner and survivor of Auschwitz, authored the acclaimed memoir, *Auschwitz and After* in which she is 'trying to invent a language of representing the horrors no one who endured them could understand as they were being perpetrated' (Lassner 182). Memory is an integral component of memoirs, and Delbo distinguishes between ordinary memory and deep memory while studying the terrors of Auschwitz:

> Ordinary memory situates the terrors of Auschwitz in the past that one has survived and from which she can separate herself because it is a thinking and analytical memory. She can now think of herself as free in a present distinct from the Holocaust past. But unlike ordinary memory, deep memory is a sensory, physical experience, and remains so much a part of the self that there is no thinking or analyzing that will allow an escape from the past. (Lassner 183 qtd. in Delbo 84)

SLAVE NARRATIVES

Slave narratives of formerly enslaved people and present-day enslaved people take different forms, such as autobiographies, biographies and oral narratives, which trace the transition of narrators from bondage to eventual freedom. Such survival stories take on a bewildering variety due to linguistic and geographical differences. As a form, slave narratives became a major corpus of African American literature, and the period from the eighteenth to the twentieth century was the time when such writings flourished. Harriet A. Jacob's *Incidents in the Life of a Slave Girl* (1861) and Frederick Douglass' *Narrative* (1845) were instrumental in popularising this form, and later, we come across neo-slave narratives, which include Richard Wright's *Black Boy* (1945) and *The Autobiography of Malcolm X* (1965), co-authored by Malcolm X and Alex Haley, followed by fictional slave narratives like Toni Morrison's *Beloved* (1987), Ernest Gaines' *The Autobiography of Miss Jane Pittman* (1971), William Wells Brown's *Clotel: Or, The President's Daughter, A Narrative of Slave Life in the United States* (1853) and Harriet Beecher Stowe's *Uncle Tom's Cabin* (1852). We can see that slave narratives highlight the aspect of ethics, since they appeal to human conscience against the cruel practice of slavery. In the case of a slave narrative by a woman, one can observe the condition of double bondage. The authenticity of a slave narrative is often questioned because of the absence of proper reference details such as birth and parentage. Indeed, some argue that slave narratives invariably instill a false sense of hope that a slave can often redeem himself from suffering. However, theoreticians including Sidonie Smith and William Andrews have categorised slave narrative as a potent form of autobiography.

Harriet A. Jacobs' *Incidents in the Life of a Slave Girl* (1861) narrates the excruciating experiences of an enslaved African American born in Edenton, North Carolina, in 1813. Having lost her parents at a young age, she and her brother were brought up by maternal grandmother, Molly Horniblow. Jacobs learned how to read, write and sew under her early mistress Margaret Horniblow, but the latter's untimely death led her to be under the control of Dr James Norcom (represented as Dr Flint in the narrative), which eventually led to a lifetime of suffering, including sexual harassment and physical abuse as a servant in the household. In order to escape the bold advances of Norcom, Jacobs fell in love with Samuel Treadwell Sawyer, a prominent white lawyer, and bore him two children, Joseph and Louisa Matilda, who legally belonged to Norcom. The narrative unfolds her separation from the children, her final escape to New York City by boat in 1842 and her reunification with Joseph and Matilda. Finally, her employer, Cornelia Grinnell Willis, purchased her freedom from the Norcoms by 1852. Harriet Jacobs' female antebellum slave narrative was published in 1861 under the pseudonym 'Linda Brent'. It projects the victimisation of enslaved African American women by white men and pitches for the importance of family and motherhood, besides addressing issues such as female bondage and sexuality from a woman's perspective, unlike the usual male-centered slave narrative genre.

FURTHER DEVELOPMENTS

The hybrid term 'auto/biography' became accepted towards the end of the twentieth century. The autobiographical mode of the early twentieth century had a confessional tone, and Oscar Wilde's *De Profundis*, in the form of a letter, traces his career as a popular figure to a miserable condition as a prisoner and details his disastrous love affair with Lord Alfred Douglas. Edmund Gosse's *Father and Son* (1907) is another autobiography with a confessional touch. World War I generated quite a few life writings based on similar lines, including Siegfried Sassoon's *Memoirs of a Fox Hunting Man* (1928), Vera Brittain's *Testament of Youth* (1933) and T. E. Lawrence's *The Seven Pillars of Wisdom* (1926).

In the modern age, women started taking a keen interest in recording their lives, and we have writers such as Sylvia Plath, Maya Angelou and Janet Frame. Maya Angelou wrote a six-volume autobiography, starting with *I Know Why The Caged Bird Sings* (1970), through which she explores the racial segregation that she encountered along with her grandmother. Family memoirs proliferated in the second half of the twentieth century, and Joseph Randolph Ackerley's *My Father and Me* (1968) is a moving example. Truman Capote popularised the new form 'non-fiction novel' through *In Cold Blood* (1966). Towards the end of the twentieth century, we come across another trend, that is, historical biographies of women. Lady Antonia Fraser's *Mary, Queen of Scots* (1969), Stella Tillyard's *Aristocrats* (1994), Amanda Foreman's *Georgiana: Duchess of Devonshire* (1998) and Amanda Vickery's *The Gentleman's Daughter: Women's Lives in Georgian England* (1998) appealed to many readers. With the popularity of second wave feminism, women wrote autobiographies debating gender identity and selfhood. Three such important works are Carolyn Steedman's *Landscape for a Good Woman* (1986), Gillian Rose's *Love's Work* (1995) and Ann Oakley's *Man and Wife* (1997) (Erben 148). Diary writing flourished in the twentieth century, particularly during World War I and Private Horace Bruckshaw (1979), the poets Siegfried Sassoon (1983) and Edward Thomas (1971) and Andrew Clark's *Echoes of the Great War* (1985) are good examples.

Writing Emotions

Life narratives are healing in nature, as they have a therapeutic effect on authors and readers; through the acts of story-telling, authors get the opportunity to unburden themselves of their traumatic experiences, whereas for the readers, it serves as a means for catharsis through the process of reading. Genres such as autobiographies, memoirs and diaries, help to heal mental wounds and tranquillise the mind. Life narratives of the victims of illnesses such as HIV/

AIDS, asthma, arthritis, etc., can help them find relief from their traumatic frame of mind. Motivational life stories bring out hope in readers to succeed against all obstacles.

Writing Death

Different forms of life writing, such as autobiographies, biographies, memoirs and obituaries, represent the various manifestations of deaths – cruel deaths due to atrocities, deaths by illnesses, etc. Nancy Miller coined the term 'autothanatographies' – 'the making public of private pain finds justification in the consciousness of bearing witness to a collective suffering that might otherwise pass unheard' (Jolly 568). Paul Monette's AIDS memoir, *Borrowed Time* (1988), recounts the premature ending of a life. We had St Augustine in the past, who narrated his mother's death in Book IX of *Confessions*, while offering a religious dimension to the loss, and a 'secular turn' in narratives of death is developed later through works such as Simone de Beauvoir's *A Very Easy Death* (1964), Virginia Woolf's recollection of her mother's deathbed in *A Sketch of the Past* (1939), and Robert Graves' World War I memoir, *Goodbye to All That* (1929). One can observe that these genres of life writing representing death perform the function of 'memorialization of the dead' (569).

An obituary is a death narrative that reports the death of a person along with a note on the person's life. Obituaries are typically published in newspapers, television channels, social media posts and message boards to inform the community of a person's death. Armando Petrucci distinguishes between an obituary and death announcement; the obituary appears as 'the memorial article that a newspaper devotes, on its own initiative, to people of particular social, political, cultural, or economic importance, while the latter was – and is – the published announcement that relatives pay for to record the disappearance of a family member and to give information on time and whereabouts of the funeral' (667). Obituaries serve different purposes: 'they inform the public of the recent loss of its citizens, honor the dead, preserve the values of the community by expounding upon the rise (and even fall) of its most famous members, and feed the desire for salacious detail by recording the life and demise of the most infamous' (668).

An obituary is a biography of an obit subject and a tribute to the deceased. An obit piece is a cultural text that performs certain functions. Individual memories of a subject are transformed into collective memories wherein everyone takes part in the loss and grief for a person who stood for certain values. The symbolic value of a subject is documented by an obituary, which turns out to be a cultural apparatus, where certain value judgements are made. The obituary text becomes a cultural text in which power relations are contested. The 'idea of class and social standing determining the amount of space the deceased is "worth" in an obituary is, of course, not a recent phenomenon.' (667). Whose life is grievable is an important issue, and the subject with cultural capital gets public visibility through obituaries. For obvious reasons, people belonging to certain subaltern groups and the lower strata get less prominence. According to the *Routledge Encyclopedia of Narrative Theory*, the 'element which distinguishes an obituary from a standard news story about death …[is] the intent of the latter to supply an account of a deceased person's life, often with information …on the circumstances of death, the obituary provides an assessment of its subject's character, achievements, and effect on society' (qtd. in Starck 5). It is interesting to note how death is narrated in an obituary. The length of an obit piece depends on a subject's social standing and cultural capital. Firstly, a subject is placed in a historical context, and then basic details such as the name, date of death, place of death, social position and other personal relations are mentioned. Very often, a photograph of the subject is included to provide immediacy.

GRAPHIC AUTO/BIOGRAPHIES

The hybrid genre of autobiographical comics became popular in the United States of America in the 1970s with the underground comics movement, and they are often subversive stories dealing with sexually explicit content for adults. Harvey Pekar's *American Splendor* (1976–2008), Art Spiegelman's *Maus* (1980–91) and Marjane Satrapi's *Persepolis* (2000) became big successes. In fact, these narratives are marked by 'taboo-breaking subject matter, subversive humor, and irony still playing a central role in many such works' (El Refaie 4). The incorporation of 'the comics medium offers new ways of telling life stories and of representing the self' (7). Speaking on the multiple potentialities of autobiographical comics, El Refaie continues:

> Creators can draw on models not only from literature but also from art and photography and their long tradition of (self) portraiture, for instance. They can also exploit the particular formal properties and sociocultural affordances of the comics medium itself, which has had a long history of marginalization but which is currently enjoying something of a cultural renaissance. (19)

In *Alternative Comics*, Charles Hatfield (2005) summarises both the centrality of autobiographical comics and the critical issues the genre raises: 'Autobiography, especially, has been central to alternative comics – whether in picaresque shaggy-dog stories or in disarmingly, sometimes harrowingly, frank uprootings of the psyche – and this has raised knotty questions about truth and fictiveness, realism and fantasy, and the relationship between author and audience' (x).

Trauma is an important aspect in many autobiographical comics, including Spiegelman's *Maus*, Satrapi's *Persepolis* and Alison Bechdel's *Fun Home* (2006). Kunka rightly observes that 'the combination of visual and verbal elements of comics can make such experiences visible to the reader' (3) and as Hillary Chute in *Graphic Women: Life Narrative and Contemporary Comics* (2010) observes, 'each ... insists on the importance of innovative textual practice offered by the rich visual-verbal form of comics to be able to represent trauma productively and ethically. For this reason, graphic narrative, invested in the ethics of testimony, assumes what I think of as the *risk of representation*.' (3)

In autobiographical comics, we can see the slipperiness of truth; as Hatfield points out, autobiography in general 'inevitably mingles the factual and the fictive' (112), but comics foreground this mingling, occasionally to the point that the only 'truth' remaining is the impossibility of total truthfulness in comics autobiography. In the year 1972, Robert Crumb created *The Confessions of R. Crumb* and Justin Green published *Binky Brown Meets the Holy Virgin*.

Autobiographical comics are 'hybrid word-and-image form[s] in which two narrative tracks, one verbal and one visual, register temporality spatially' (Chute, *Comics as Literature* 452). Female comic artists have also made significant contributions to the field of autobiographical comics and we come across writers such as Aline Kominsky and Phoebe Gloeckner. Early childhood experiences and family life form a major component of many autobiographical comics including Al Davidson's *The Spiral Cage: An Autobiography* (1988). The centrality of the body is an important aspect of autobiographical comics and multiple layers of the self are drawn. Many autobiographical comics deal with illness and disability. The graphic memoirs offer opportunities to 'ordinary' people who 'nevertheless have extraordinary tales to tell, for instance, about their experiences of living with a disability, surviving a serious illness, or suffering bereavement' (El Refaie 222).

The basic element is the panel (or frame) which defines (establishes) and fractures both time and space (McCloud 67). The arrangement of panels textures the grid of the page. One panel is separated from the next by the gutter. Panels are inhabited by icons; they are endowed with sound through word balloons and sound effects (icons indicating sound); they may or may not contain words in speech balloons (by the characters) or captions (by the narrator) (Wagner-Egelhaaf 443). Kukkonen posits three autographic agents: 'the narrator, who creates the image; the focalizer, on whose knowledge it is based; and the observer, whose embodied spatial position is represented and which the reader is invited to share' (59). Autobiographical/autofictional comics very often 'follow an agenda that often puts socially marginalized issues center stage' (68). For instance, in Joe Sacco (*Palestine* [1993], *Footnotes in Gaza* [2009]), the 'medium of comics can perform the enabling political and aesthetic work of bearing witness powerfully because of its rich narrative texture' (Chute, *Graphic Women* 4). In graphic autobiographies and memoirs, photographs are used as a powerful narrative mode because they help in 'performing authenticity' (El Refaie 159) while drawing photographs 'within the story world' (158). She continues, 'Unlike most of the more common comics genres, graphic memoirs frequently include photographic images and other forms of "documentary evidence" in their work, either in their "pure" form or in a graphic rendering' (158).

Comics as a medium are used to write and draw about diseases, and we call such forms 'graphic medicine'. Drawing one's sick body over again and again 'provides the opportunity for them to engage explicitly with their own body images and with the sociocultural assumptions and values that render bodies meaningful' (91), as El Refaie explains what she refers to as 'pictorial embodiment' (51).

DISABILITY LIFE WRITING

Impairment/disability

Impairment is physical whereas disability is essentially a social position resulting from a prejudice against the ill. In fact, we may consider disability life narratives counter-narratives or counter-stories because they are written from the perspective of the marginalised. We may consider Helen Keller's text 'a critique of a world designed, built and maintained for the non-disabled. The fundamental distinction in critical disability studies between impairment, which is found in the body, and disability, which is located in the environment, has begun to be exposed in life writing' (Couser, "Signifying Selves" 201).

There is growing interest among readers and publishers alike in the field of disability life narratives representing different types of illnesses including amputation, amyotrophic lateral sclerosis (also known as Lou Gehrig's disease), anorexia, anxiety, asthma, bipolar illness and borderline personality disorder. It may be added here that cyberspace offers plenty opportunities for self-publishing, with the additional advantage of a decrease in publication costs. Besides these, blogs and other social networking groups give support and popularity to these ventures as well. Disability life writings motivate readers and those suffering from various physical illnesses to fight against all adversities. However, writers such as Couser argue that such narratives have a negative side too, as they offer '(false) reassurance to the nondisabled' with the 'rhetoric of triumph' (203). The problem happens while narrating 'the position of the narrator whose condition is permanent or even progressive' which denies a natural happy ending (205). Couser continues:

> Granted, happy endings are typical of most autobiography and memoir, because few people relish writing self-narratives with downward narrative arcs. Narratives that offer up unlikely supercrips (a disparaging term for disabled people who overcompensate for their supposed deficiencies) are often referred to by disabled people as "inspiration porn" because in *life*, as distinct from life writing, such triumph is the exception rather than the rule. (203)

Another problematic issue is the question of agency, because 'cognitive, neurological, and physical impairments may make it difficult or impossible for disabled people to speak for themselves, much less to represent themselves in print' (207). In such cases, assistive technology or mediators can play a major role in empowering the subject. In unfortunate situations, those who write/narrate on behalf of disabled subjects may misinterpret or distort reality, which is unethical.

Alzheimer's disease life writings or dementia narratives have become popular and we have excellent examples such as J. Bernlef's *Out of Mind* (1989), Robert Davis' *My Journey into Alzheimer's Disease* (1989) and Diana Friel McGowin's *Living in the Labyrinth* (1993). In fact, they can be categorised as caregiver narratives as they illustrate patients' traumatic experiences documented by their caregivers. There is obviously memory loss in the narrative, 'suggesting that identity is lost in Alzheimer's disease, and subjectivity is altered' (Zimmermann 8). However, one cannot overlook the ethical implications of dementia life writing because a caregiver's agenda may not always be in conjunction with the patient's outlook given the fact that 'patients themselves cannot write about their experiences in the final stages of the condition' (13).

The writers of disability life stories narrate the lives of their subjects by occupying a precarious subject position; they can only write 'on behalf' of their subjects, and quite naturally, their ideological predilections and personal agendas colour their observations. Speaking on this aspect of disability autobiographies in his book, Couser makes the following observation:

> Disability autobiographers typically begin from a position of marginalization, belatedness, and pre-inscription. Long the objects of others' classification and examination, disabled people have only recently assumed the initiative in representing themselves; in disability autobiography particularly, disabled people counter their historical objectification (or even abjection) by occupying the subject position. The representation of disability in such narratives is thus a political as well as a mimetic act-a matter of speaking *for* as well as speaking *about*. (*Signifying Bodies* 7)

Couser further argues that disability life writings are essentially postcolonial and even anticolonial in nature, and he quotes Mary Louise Pratt's comment on it: 'instances in which colonized subjects undertake to represent themselves in ways that *engage with* [read: contest] the colonizer's own terms' (7). It is a fact that Western culture has given us a distorted or prejudiced inscription/representation of the body not just along the lines of identity markers such as gender, race and sexuality but also 'along the lines of those somatic conditions we call illness and disability' (9) through narratives like different genres of literature and media including life writing. Thus, we see representations of some characters as crippled or maimed, such as Melville's Ahab. Couser continues: 'Western culture, both high and low, often pre-inscribes narratives on the bodies of people with aberrant somatic conditions, willy-nilly' (18).

Performative Utterances

Memoir is a popular form and memoirs act as performative utterances. Here, we may cite Helen Keller's autobiography, *The Story of My Life* (1903) as a good example. A few more examples are Anna Agnew's *From under the Cloud; or, Personal Reminiscences of Insanity* (1887), Hiram Chase's *Two Years and Four Months in a Lunatic Asylum* (1868) and Moses Swan's *Ten Years and Ten Months in Lunatic Asylums in Different States* (1874). Such narratives reconfigure traditional social attitudes towards the disabled and even strongly critique dominant narratives about them. Couser observes: 'The fundamental distinction in critical disability studies between impairment, which is found in the body, and disability, which is located in the environment, has begun to be exposed in life writing ("Signifying Selves" 201). Lorraine Adams classifies disability memoirs into 'somebody' memoirs and 'nobody' memoirs. Somebody memoirs are written by celebrities and they have 'the advantage of a preexisting audience: the narrative is a consequence of and a capitalisation on their fame. In contrast, nobody memoirs have to earn their audiences on their own merits: if their hitherto anonymous authors achieve fame, it is a function of their stories attracting readers' (202).

LIFE WRITING AND CULTURAL STUDIES

Life writing and cultural studies intersect on certain points; for instance, both fields subscribe to 'the concept of the constructedness of culture/s' (Wagner-Egelhaaf 35). Here, Judith Butler's notion of gender performativity plays a pivotal role in autobiographical studies. Identity politics is the crucial factor here, as are also the mechanisms of its cultural inscription through writing, particularly through the myriad modes of life narrative. 'The autobiography, for a long time already, is deemed to be the anthropological project par excellence of the modern era, where subjectivity is tested as a project' (35). Life writings in general inscribe the lives of subjects in specific sociocultural contexts, and it is natural that such texts are also commentaries on certain cultural happenings, particularly while explaining the role of individual subjects behind them. In postcolonial life writings, we see how postcolonial subjectivities are constructed, challenging the hegemonic colonial ideology. In the postcolonial context, women have successfully empowered themselves by narrating their selves through Western forms such as autobiographies, diaries, etc. The marginalised groups in society, the so-called subalterns, too, write their lives, through autobiographies, testimonies, and other genres. Testimonies and autobiographies of tribals and Dalits are aplenty, and those texts, in general, construct a collective identity, with narrators telling stories on behalf of a community. C. K. Janu, a tribal leader in Kerala, wrote *Mother Forest*, a tale of the *paniyar*, her tribal group. The same is the case with most Dalit autobiographies.

The question of identity formation can be closely connected with memory studies, and researchers such as Aleida Assmann and Jan Assmann have exposed its possibilities by highlighting the aspect of cultural remembering. Remembering is a mode of identity formation and literature in general, and the forms of life writing particularly narrate different versions of memory by archiving the past. As Max Saunders observes: 'If other genres or sub-genres or forms can be read as life writing, such as novels, poems, short stories, travel writing, topographical books, historiography – they can all be used as routes into cultural memory' (322). He continues: 'our memories are always already textualized' (322). By definition, they are 'after the event,… as representations or mediations or narrativizations of the event, they have always begun to turn the event into something else' (323). Since memories are mediated, literature, through its multiple forms, does offer some version of cultural memory, though we may not claim the facts and authenticity of the experiences recounted. However, Saunders brings out the possibilities of life writing thus: 'studying literary life-writing texts as sources for cultural memory can make us more sophisticated cultural historians, and more sophisticated students of memory' (323).

REFERENCES

Adams, Lorraine. "Almost Famous: The Rise of the 'Nobody' Memoir." *Washington Monthly*, 1 April 2001, https://washingtonmonthly.com/2001/04/01/almost-famous/. Accessed 24 April 2024.

Chute, Hillary. *Graphic Women: Life Narrative and Contemporary Comics.* Columbia UP, 2010.

---. "Comics as Literature? Reading Graphic Narrative." *PMLA* 123.2 (2008): pp. 452–465.

Couser, Thomas G. *Signifying Bodies: Disability in Contemporary Life Writing.* The U of Michigan P, 2012.

---. "Signifying Selves: Disability and Life Writing" in *The Cambridge Companion to Literature and Disability*, edited by Clare Barker and Stuart Murray. Cambridge UP, 2017.

Delbo, Charlotte. *Auschwitz and After*, translated by Rosette C. Lamont. Yale U P, 1995.

Erben, Michael. "Britain: 20th Century Auto/ biography." *Encyclopedia of Life Writing: Autobiographical and Biographical Forms Volume 1*, edited by Margaretta Jolly. Fitzroy Dearborn Publishers, 2001.

El Refaie, Elisabeth. *Autobiographical Comics: Life Writing in Pictures*. UP of Mississippi, 2012.

Hartman, Geoffrey. *The Longest Shadow: In the Aftermath of the Holocaust*. Palgrave, 1996.

Hatfield, C. *Alternative Comics: An Emerging Literature*. UP of Mississippi, 2005.

Jolly, Margaretta, editor. *Encyclopedia of Life Writing: Autobiographical and Biographical Forms Volume 1*. Fitzroy Dearborn Publishers, 2001.

Kukkonen, Karin. *Studying Comics and Graphic Novels*. Wiley Blackwell, 2013.

Kunka, Andrew J. *Autobiographical Comics*. Bloomsbury, 2018.

Lassner, Phyllis. "Life Writing and the Holocaust." Marina Mackay, editor, *The Cambridge Companion to the Literature of World War II*. Cambridge UP, 2009.

McCloud, Scott. *Understanding Comics. The Invisible Art*. Harper Perennial, 1994.

Petrucci, Armando. *Writing the Dead: Death and Writing Strategies in the Western Tradition*. Translated by Michael Sullivan. Stanford UP, 1988.

Pratt, Mary Louise. *Imperial Eyes: Travel Writing and Transculturation*. Routledge, 1992.

Saunders, Max. "Life-Writing, Cultural Memory and Literary Studies." *Cultural Memory Studies: An International and Interdisciplinary Handbook*, edited by Astrid Erll, Ansgar Nünning, Sara B. Young. Walter de Gruyter, 2008.

Starck, Nigel. *Life After Death: The Art of Obituary*. Carlton, 2006.

Wagner-Egelhaaf, Martina, editor. *Handbook of Autobiography/Autofiction*. De Gruyter, 2017.

Zimmermann, Martina. *The Poetics and Politics of Alzheimer's Disease Life - Writing*. Palgrave Macmillan, 2017.

Chapter Four

Postcolonial Life Writing

INTRODUCTION

Postcolonial thinkers such as Benedict Anderson, Edward Said and Homi Bhabha, among others, have conceived of the nation as a narrative construct and credited literature with playing a significant role in imagining and constructing postcolonial national identities. Herein lies the relevance of the non-fictional form, life writing, a relatively modern development in configuring national identities. With the wave of globalisation and its concomitant border-crossings, the nation is obviously a major concern in the realm of life writing. In fact, life writing occupies a precarious and slippery position in this aspect: on the one hand, it inscribes the politically dominant nation state, but on the other, it welcomes voices from the margins. In this context, Betty Ann Bergland comments: 'on the one hand, the nation is seen as the legitimate form of political authority, yet on the other hand, challenges to the sovereignty of the nation persist, driven by varied forces - the globalized economy, information technologies, migration of labour, refugee displacements, and the ongoing effects of postcolonialism' (Jolly 636).

Ever since countries were freed from the colonial yoke, there has been a surge in the field of life writing, including life narratives from places such as the Caribbean, Africa, India, etc. One of the main concerns in all such postcolonial narratives is the dilemma of using the language of the coloniser. Postcolonial life writing also has the political agenda of inscribing liminal identities and documenting the voices of the subaltern, and we have seen some bold academic initiatives such as the Subaltern Studies Collective headed by

Ranajit Guha. It may be admitted that the relatively vast corpus of life writing has been a useful mode of understanding history from a different angle, offering new platforms for fresh interpretations within the already existing corpus of historiography.

DECENTRED SUBJECTIVITIES

The inscription of decentred subjectivities can be seen in postcolonial life writings. Ashcroft, Griffiths and Tiffin (1989) and some other postcolonial theorists argue that a major concern of postcolonial writings in general is dislocation and identity crisis. 'It is here that the special postcolonial crisis of identity comes into being; the concern with the development or recovery of an effective identifying relationship between self and place' (Ashcroft, Griffiths and Tiffin 8–9). Moore-Gilbert argues that both male and female postcolonial life writers adopt both models of selfhood – centered and decentered (16). Fanon has argued that rewriting selfhood acts as a powerful remedy against psychic disintegration caused by colonialism.

According to Brodzki and Schenck, 'Self-definition in relation to significant others, is the most pervasive characteristic of the female autobiography' (qtd. in Evans 83). Salman Rushdie's *Midnight's Children* (1981) starts both with the 'birth' of the Indian nation on 15 August 1947 and the birth of its protagonist: 'I was born [...] on August 15th, 1947 [...]. On the stroke of midnight [...]. [At] the precise instant of India's arrival at independence, I tumbled forth into the world' (Rushdie 1). Rushdie's protagonist, Saleem, is thus 'mysteriously handcuffed to history' (3). Postcolonial literature can be considered 'a form of cultural and political rebirth' (Wagner-Egelhaaf 130). It also serves as a statement of intellectual and cultural independence, which stems from the severance of all bonds with the imperial regime. Slowly, like Shakespeare's Caliban, the erstwhile othered colonies in the periphery have declared freedom through the performative act of writing back to the centre. Obviously, it is all about 'shifting of perspective, and a critical – and literary – practice that sets out to unearth cultural legacies which have been submerged by British colonial power' (131).

Western metaphysics has always privileged unified, centred subjects, and according to Evans, this 'project of masculinity emphasizes … the completed self' (Evans 6). Moore-Gilbert further adds that 'women's life-writing has traditionally been marginalised within the male-dominated formation of Auto/biography Studies' (1). However, postmodernism celebrates decentring of subject, and postcolonial life writing also subscribes to this viewpoint. Interestingly, in *Out of Place*, Edward Said argues: 'I occasionally experience myself as a cluster of flowing currents. I prefer this to the idea of a solid self, the identity to which so many attach so much significance' (295). Postcolonial auto/biographical subjectivity, on the other hand, embodies the effects of colonialism; it can either refuse to integrate with the alien culture or fuse with colonial culture to form a hybrid identity (Moore-Gilbert 15). Women who write their life histories inscribe not only their individual stories alone but also their collective/gendered histories; the individual self is often related to others, and in this process, a collective identity is formed.

There have been heated debates over the colonial agenda behind the introduction of auto/biographical forms in the non-Western world. Critics such as Gusdorf point out the success of the West's imperial project, indeed, somewhat ominously suggesting that the genre has 'been of good use in [the West's] systematic conquest of the universe' (Moore-Gilbert xii). In *Design and Truth in Autobiography* (1960), Roy Pascal argues that 'autobiography is essentially European' (Moore-Gilbert 22). However, Moore-Gilbert hints at Gandhi's obvious disavowal of the form of autobiography and argues that it is not a new phenomenon in non-Western countries. Janet Gunn argued how 'Third World autobiography' is different from Western autobiography in two ways: 'First it involves an unmasking or what I have called a denostalgizing of the past; second, it orients itself towards a liberated society in the future. In the first respect, it is a form of resistance literature; in the second, it is a form of utopian literature' (77). Moore-Gilbert argues that 'postcolonial life-writing has sometimes advanced conceptions of personhood that are highly culturally specific' (xx). In order to understand Gandhi's *An*

Autobiography, it is important to understand his Hindu background. Therefore, the 'ideological I' (Smith and Watson 81) is a significant one in postcolonial subjectivity formation.

JOOTHAN

Joothan (2003), an autobiography by Omprakash Valmiki, depicts the Dalits' plight in independent India. The term 'joothan' refers to food left on an eater's plate, which is representative of the downtrodden class' life of pain and humiliation. The author's childhood experiences in Barla village, his student days, his career as a government servant, and later as an activist are all covered in the autobiography, which is divided into four sections. The life-text addresses issues like caste domination, poverty, and the restriction of Dalit education, among others. Valmiki's autobiography is a protest narrative aimed at reclaiming and redefining the Dalit identity.

SHORT TAKES

POSTCOLONIAL AUTO/BIOGRAPHY

Postcolonialism has the political agenda to dismantle the dominant, hegemonic knowledge system of the coloniser and autobiography is a popular genre which helps in deconstructing the imperial project. Autobiography emerged in the West to celebrate essentialist, white and unified selves, and later postcolonial life writings positively challenged this enlightenment rationalised notion of self. Fanon's struggle to hold on to the enlightenment idea of the human – even when he knew that European imperialism had reduced that idea to the figure of the settler-colonial white man – is now itself part of the global heritage of all postcolonial thinkers (Chakrabarty 5). Linda Anderson links autobiography to the 'essentialist or romantic notions of selfhood' (4). According to this perspective, which emerged in the late-eighteenth century and persisted until the mid-twentieth century, 'each individual possesses a unified, unique selfhood which is also the expression of a universal human nature' (5). Sidonie Smith and Julia Watson argue that traditionally, autobiography has been privileged over various forms of life writings including diaries, memoirs, or testimonies, attributing them to 'lesser value' (Whitlock 3).

Autobiography as a genre emerged as 'simultaneously too abstract, too masculine, and Western' (Huddart 2), appealing to the middle class. Anderson suggests that, 'Insofar as autobiography has been seen as promoting a view of the subject as universal, it has also underpinned the centrality of masculine – and, we may add, Western and middle-class – modes of subjectivity' (Anderson 2). It challenges and questions all sorts of power structures, including 'a response to neo-colonial structures' (3). However, Hornung and Ruhe argue that 'Autobiography in its widest definition seems to provide a convenient genre to embrace the crossroad cultures from East and West and to launch an emancipatory political and cultural program' (3).

SHORT TAKES

AUTOBIOGRAPHY AS DE-FACEMENT

Paul de Man's important essay 'Autobiography as De-facement' (1979) offers a deconstructive reading of autobiography in the context of analysing William Wordsworth's critical work *Essays upon Epitaphs*. To him, autobiography is inherently unstable and is not a genre but only a figure of reading. It is difficult to fix an autobiographical text in a particular historical context. In fact, the life inscribed in an autobiography may not necessarily be the one which is lived by the author.

Several critics of autobiography, including the French critic Phillipe Lejeune have stressed the literality of autobiography as a form. However, because of its so-called 'political' dimension in the wake of decolonisation and postcolonialism with the subsequent focus on the subaltern, autobiography as a genre becomes crucial in the entire corpus of postcolonial literature, where genres such as fiction, poetry and drama rule the roost. 'More than a mere representation of one's life, autobiographical writings are a powerful quest for identity, for self-knowledge and self-recognition, particularly meaningful in colonial and postcolonial times' (Lebdai 2). In fact, the form 'ponders broader social and psychological issues in postcoloniality' (2).

Many critics, including Lionnet and Moore-Gilbert argue that postcolonial life writing as a whole can be defined only by individual subjects and their respective communities. Here, it is important to quote G. N. Devy who links individual identity with nation, race, or ethnicity, and he continues: 'if a [postcolonial Indian] writer cannot relate himself meaningfully to his culture, his society, the whole purpose of writing an autobiography is lost. Such a book ... cannot succeed in creating organic links with the society which should be the aim of an autobiography' (65).

Life writers employ visual texts such as photographs to narrate their past lives, and one can observe the play of ideology in 'the act of posing for and taking photographs, and the act of looking at photographs' (Kim 402). Here, memory plays a major role in 'the processes of remembering, recollecting, interpreting, and reconstructing' (402) the past. In fact, postcolonial subjects can make use of this trope 'in registering, and at times dramatising, the struggles....in writing about their childhoods and familial relationships' (401).

Moore-Gilbert argues that the body, 'an important thematic of some auto/biographical subjectivity' (35) is relatively unexplored in auto/biography studies. Apart from its discursive aspect, body's materiality too helps in the formation of identity (48). He adds: "female auto/biographers have found the body to provide rich grounds for thinking through the relationship between identity and representation" (7). Sidonie Smith too claims that '[S]ome kind of history of the body is always inscribed in women's autobiographical texts' (Smith and Watson 35). According to Fedwa Malti-Douglas, for feminists, the body is 'a physical reality that in itself possesses no necessary moral or social meaning but is then invested with a moral value. This investment, in turn, dictates social conclusions' (qtd. in Smith and Watson 35).

A body is defined in the context of its location and topography. In the context of women's life writing, Moore-Gilbert observes: 'women's subjectivities are partly determined by their insertion within a variety of socio-spatial locations. In descending order of scale, these range from global diasporas, through nation spaces, cities and rural areas to domestic dwellings and, indeed, the Body' (51).

TESTIMONIES AS RESISTANCE

Postcolonial autobiographies have decolonised the form of autobiography and specific forms such as the testimonial, which 'speaks on behalf of a collective rather than the singular authoritative "I"' (Whitlock 5). A very special aspect of testimonial narratives is that they embody 'social activism' (5) as they speak on behalf of vulnerable subjects such as slaves or rape victims. Testimonial narratives address 'the codification of human rights' (8) and, in fact, they 'appeal to an addressee, a text in search of a witness, a desire to invoke witnessing publics' (8). While discussing the purpose of testimonials, Felman and Laub argue:

> The specific task of literary testimony is, in other words, to open up in that belated witness, which the reader now historically becomes, the imaginative capacity of perceiving history—what is happening to others—*in one's own body*, with the power of sight (of insight) usually afforded only by one's own immediate physical involvement. (10)

As in life narratives, testimonies are performative as they 'summon and beseech us readers'(Whitlock 8), and establish emotional entanglements between the protagonists and the readers, who bear witness to excruciating experiences in the text, and one can witness the note of dissent or resistance in such narratives, even against colonisation and other injustices. However, testimonies can 'move the reader and produce collective "witnessing publics", but these are temporary and contingent collectives hailed through rhetorical address, an active engagement and responsibility that is subject to change' (Torchin 14).

SHORT TAKES

TESTIMONIO

Emerging from early slave narratives, testimonio/testimony was a Latin American form of life writing which became popular in 1960s and continued till 1990s, by narrators belonging to the margins of society including women, peasants, etc. Testimonials could be book-length narratives written by others on behalf of the subjects, wherein readers encounter the injustices and human rights violations experienced by the subjects. Testimonios are political as well as literary narratives that 'tell the story of exploitation, oppression and resistance from the point of view of those exploited who resist and fight against oppression and exploitation' (Jolly 670). The existing social structures of exploitation are attacked in this genre and social change is anticipated for good. Apart from being individual life stories, testimonios acquire a collective identity and they speak on behalf of a suffering group such as peasants, miners, slaves, women and others. Miguel Barnet's *Biography of A Runaway Slave* is regarded as the first testimonio. Elena Poniatowska's *Massacre in Mexico* (1971), and *I, Rigoberta Menchú: An Indian Woman in Guatemala* (1984) etc., are some other powerful testimonios.

Whitlock categorises Dalit personal narratives as part of testimonial culture, as they offer resistance against caste hegemony and discrimination, appealing to basic human rights on an international level. Srinivasan highlights the political agenda involved in it:

> When Dalit writing features in comparative and transnational studies, it bodes well for the Dalit cause and the future of Dalit writing. We are positioned at that point in history when the strategy of internationalising Dalit issues is on the political agenda of the Dalit people. This being the case, a transnational linkage between Australian Aboriginal writer Jackie Huggins and Indian Dalit feminists, Bama and Kumud Pawde is indeed appropriate. (98–99)

Indigenous forms of life writing, particularly testimonies in the postcolonial context, offer a counter-discursive mode of narrating the nation, as opposed to the dominant, official interpretation. 'Indigenous writing troubles the limited and provisional citizenship and belonging that becomes available to indigenous peoples in nation and narration' (Whitlock 138). As a matter of fact, testimonial narratives are 'specific kinds of cultural recall' (138) which construct a counter-memory by reconfiguring history. However, 'memory is a cultural phenomenon, as well as an individual and social one, and the acts of recall that are elicited in testimonial cultures are performative and polemical acts in pursuit of social justice' (138). An individual's identity is marked by how he interacts in his sociocultural contexts, and different 'cultures require different forms of thick description in order to capture their different ethical orientations' (Huddart 2). He brings in the notion of 'cultural relativity' (1) and argues that 'I say things about my social, cultural, or ethical identity within a context or framework of questions' (1).

SHORT TAKES

I, RIGOBERTA MENCHÚ

I, Rigoberta Menchú (1984) is a famous testimony of Rigoberta Menchú, a Mayan woman from Guatemala who received the Nobel Peace Prize in 1992 for her human rights activism in her country. In her life narrative, she exposes the brutal suppression of the indigenous Guatemalans by the ruling class and the Guatemalan government. The book holds a mirror to the world about how a group of people were subjected to exploitation and mistreatment by the authorities. Written with the power of the rhetoric, the testimony raises the voice of the Guatemalan peasants to reclaim their culture.

To put it in brief, the different modes of postcolonial life writing have been decolonising/debunking and deconstructing the 'sovereign' subject of the dominant paradigm of the West by opening up a democratic space where multiple and othered voices are heard widely and rather vociferously.

LIFE WRITING IN SOUTH ASIA

There is an increase in the production and distribution of various forms of life writing, particularly in South Asia. Many factors have contributed to this relatively new trend, including the fact that most countries that gained independence while under colonial control invariably constructed or imagined national identities, and forms of life story invariably constructed or imagined national identities. In many ways, such writings highlight the aspect of resistance to colonisers' oppression. We can see contemporary forms such as blogs and YouTube where individual and collective memories are stored for future generations as a result of the digital revolution and the impact of technical growth. Furthermore, self-publication allows individuals to publish their writings without having to wait for permission from publishers.

Life writing emerges from various sites of South Asian trauma, such as partition, emergency and the Sri Lankan civil war, among various others. It is no surprise that traumatic memories are prevalent in a wide range of works and narratives, including autobiographies, memoirs, testimonials, films, documentaries, and so on. The theme of survival appears in several writings, notably those of Malala Yousafzai and Taslima Nasrin, and it serves to empower future generations. Several groups of subalterns, including women, Dalits, adivasis, and other oppressed sections of society, express their discontentment with oppression and demand basic human rights and living dignity through their narratives.

Writing lives, on the other hand, is a 'trend' among society's elite; many successful individuals, politicians, bureaucrats and other celebrities describe their success tales and receive a large number of readers. In some cases, such acts of self-promotion take the form of biopics, particularly among sports or film personalities with widespread public appeal. Many of these narratives are spoken and mediated, and we can witness a new generation of writers writing on their behalf. There are also ghost writers who work in the background, writing for others. The voyeurism of readers to peep into people's lives can be a major reason behind the popularity of life narratives across the world and in South Asia in particular.

LIFE HISTORIES IN INDIA

Telling lives through auto/biographies, novels, poems, folktales, etc., has been a human urge since time immemorial, and different cultures adopt different genres for self-enunciation. In India, there was an early tendency among life historians to select the so-called 'great' and 'famous' as their subjects, glorifying their deeds, but subsequently, since 1990, focus has also shifted to subaltern subjects, and we have James M. Freeman's account of Muli, the untouchable in Odisha, as a counterpoint to David G. Mandelbaum's account of Gandhi. Individual agency was kept subservient to collective identities, and David Arnold and Stuart Blackburn introduce the 'paradigm of collectivity' (2) and continue to observe: '... it was frequently assumed that caste was one of the essential attributes of Indian society and that identities founded on caste and religion dominated to such a degree that individual agency and a sense of selfhood (and hence life histories and other individualistic modes of expression) were marginal to South Asian thought and behaviour' (2). In India, society was glorified, if not individuals (Dirks 57). However, Arnold and Blackburn introduce two assumptions about life history research: one is about veracity, or the capacity of life narratives to include some elements of truth; and second, 'personal lives reflect culture-specific notions of the person or self' (4), as they are 'valuable sources for understanding the emergence of a modern sense of self, of individualism and self-consciousness as opposed to collective identity' (5). Thus, we can see that the self in the Indian context was tied to different levels of identity, such as caste, religion, or community, and the individual self was not foregrounded at all.

Many religious traditions and regional cultures in India, such as Buddhism, Islam, Christianity, Hinduism, and others, have generated a wide range of life histories, which are written, oral or graphic in nature. The biography of Shakyamuni Buddha was narrated in both Pali and Sanskrit narratives, and his life from Bodhisattva to enlightenment was visually depicted in Buddhist temple didactic iconography from the second century onwards. In pre-modern India, life histories were recorded in a variety of ways, including genealogy and horoscopes, which were both oral and written down. The majority of them were hagiographical – oral and written descriptions of deities, kings, cultural heroes, saints, poet-gods and poet-kings' lives. There was a tendency to glorify the subjects and position the narrative within a mythic framework, and such narratives were written in either prose or verse, evidently with differing points of view. Supernatural events, dreams, prophesies, vows and divine intercession were used to explain events in the poet's or hero's lives. Many of these people's lives have been canonised or anthologised.

KATHAPRASANGAM

Kathaprasangam is a twentieth-century performative art form based on stories from Indian epics and Puranas that originated in Kerala. In fact, it is a unique type of storytelling in which the storyteller, *kathikan*, engages in speaking, acting and singing. The performances began on temple grounds during festival seasons and later at social gatherings, but they were largely secular in nature, with songs, stories and biographical descriptions narrated while delivering dramatic tales. Storytelling by stalwarts like Kedamangalam Sadanandan, V. Sambasivan, Paravur Sukumaran and others, which originated in Harikathakalashepam, has succeeded in propagating progressive views in Kerala society.

HARSHACHARITA

Harshacharita (The Life of Harsha) is a seventh-century Sanskrit biography of Harsha, the Buddhist emperor of North India, written by Banabhatta. In fact, *charita* is a primordial form of biography in the Indian context, not essentially Western in form at all. Written in an ornate, poetic style, the life writer's approach is hagiographic, mixing facts with fiction. However, *Harshacharita* is divided into eight chapters and it gives us some valuable details regarding rural life in India during that period as well as the royal dynasty. The biography was later translated into English in 1897 by Edward Byles Cowell and Frederick William Thomas.

HARIKATHA

Harikatha (the story of Hari, the Lord) is a South Indian narrative storytelling style that emerged during the twelfth-century Bhakti movement. The storyteller usually narrates the life of a saint or a story from an Indian epic, which is usually accompanied by songs and music. Mullukutla Sadasiva Sastry of Tenali is well-known for his Harikatha rendering of Saint Tyagaraja's life. The purpose of this traditional Indian life narrative is to teach specific cultural and religious ideals as well as show people the path of liberation.

With the arrival of Islam, a number of life-history forms from the Middle East and Central Asia began to be adopted, including the lives of Sufi pirs and ghazis, whose tombs became sites of reverence, leading to the spread of legends about them. The early Mughal rulers were encouraged by Indo-Persian tradition to write autobiographical memoirs, beginning with the *Baburnama* in the sixteenth century and later the *Akbarnama*. In Islamic South Asia, however, a tradition of religious biography or 'lives as lessons', had become widespread. Throughout the nineteenth century, missionaries and their converts disseminated tales of Christ's life, as well as those of Christian saints and heroes, adding to the already diversified nature of life stories and exemplary biographies (Arnold and Blackburn 8).

During the colonial period, the hagiographical tradition was displaced by a new kind of biography that emphasised character complexity and personal drive, as well as specific places and events and how they contributed to the formation of a personality. Traditional legends and fables gave way to 'history' as a result of contact with European ideals and education. The advent of commercial printing boosted the production and distribution of life histories and other small biographies of mostly brilliant men and women, both Western and Indian. They took on a hagiographic form and style, and their titles frequently included the word *charita*. The lives of gods and saints, warrior heroes and political leaders, and even ordinary men and women, were all shown in Indian cinema. With the release of books by Mohandas Karamchand Gandhi and Jawaharlal Nehru around this time, autobiographical writings became popular. Court chronicles became popular throughout the Mughal period, but a surge of biographical writing flourished during British India, focusing on the British Empire's founders and guardians. Typical Indian biographies, that is, lives of Indians written by Indians, have been published since the 1870s, and Swadesabhimani K. Ramakrishnapillai penned the first biography of Karl Marx in an Indian language in 1912. Other notable biographies from this period include Meer Ali's *Life of Muhammad* (1873), Kshetrapal Chakravarthy's *Life of Sri Chaitanya* (1897), P. C. Ray's *Life and Times of C. R. Das* (1927), R. P. Paranjape's *Life of G. K. Gokhale* (1915) and H. P. Mody's *Sir Pherozshah Mehta* (1921) (Vijayasree 11-14).

Udaya Kumar identifies 'a range of motivations' (13) behind the emergence of autobiographical texts in the Indian context: 'Devotional enthusiasm, spiritual and ethical practices, testimonies in law courts, administrative documentation, political participation, and historical witnessing were perhaps the most obvious driving forces' (13). He puts forward two features of modern Indian autobiography:

> Indian autobiographies from the nineteenth and twentieth centuries, especially those written by men, rarely speak of private interiorities: self-narration in them is seldom confessional intimacy. Second, the distinctiveness of the individual life is not the focal point of most such texts. It is, in fact, as if the author's distinctive life were a pretext for revealing something more typical or larger' (14).

Whether there was an indigenous tradition of life writing in India before the emergence of the Western genres in the modern sense is a debatable issue, and historians such as Vijaya Ramaswamy contend that 'self-reflexive writing in the autobiographical mode has long been a part of Indian literary tradition' (Ramaswamy and Sharma 1) and call such writings 'autobiographies in palimpsest' (3). Banabhatta's *Harshachrita* from the seventh century is regarded as one of the earliest biographies written in India, much before the advent of colonial rule. Another indication of the existence of biographical tradition in the early period is Sandhyakaranandin's *Ramacharitam* of the eleventh and twelfth centuries. It may be noted that all these works are fictionalised accounts of lives interspersed with facts and rooted in hagiographic tradition. Another crucial early biography is *Madhura Vijayam* by Ganga Devi, the wife of Kumara Kampana of Vijayanagar written around the fifteenth century.

There are plenty of examples of political profiles and biographies glorifying British administrators, both by Westerners and Indians. Philip Woodruff's *Men Who Ruled India* and S. Gopal's biographies of Lord Ripon and Lord Irwin are good instances here. However, the deliberate 'silence' followed by the biographies in leaving out the dark episodes in a subject's life is in tune with our hagiographic tradition. At the same time, Ramaswamy argues that there are grains of truth in biographical accounts of 'people in the middle' (9). We have Banarasidas' biography, *Ardhakathanaka*, which throws light on the medieval world of business, Sethu Ramaswamy's *Bride at Ten, Mother at Fifteen*, and the life of Viramma, a Dalit woman, as good examples.

We can thus see that biographical writings existed hundreds of years ago in India in the form of stories such as the encomiastic Jataka tales, recounting the various incarnations of Lord Buddha, albeit they may not have been in the current form. According to Devy, the 'artist had practised, very rigorously, a strategy of self-effacement' in which the ego was regarded as 'just an infinitesimal fraction of the brahman' (81). The Bhakti tradition, which promotes self-assertion for renunciation, eventually overtook the Brahminical practise of self-abnegation, and contemporary autobiography evolved in the nineteenth century as part of colonial modernity. However, early autobiographies, such as Manibhai Nabhubhai's Gujarati autobiography *Atmarrutant* from the nineteenth century, show a combination of subgenres of life writing, including journals, diaries, letters and testimonials.

Bhimayana

The caste politics of Indian society are exposed in *Bhimayana: Experiences of Untouchability* (2011), which was written by Srividya Natarajan and S. Anand and featured illustrations by Durgabai and Subhash Vyam. As a matter of fact, it 'is not only a graphic representation of the life of B. R. Ambedkar, a key player in the unification and mobilisation of the Dalits, but creates a critical literacy about caste through its multimodal semiotic strategies, making us meta-aware to the positions not just within the text but also to situations without' (Chakraborty 1). *Bhimayana* is not only a graphic novel, but also a biography in its own right. The authors use Gond art to illustrate Bhim's experiences of violence and untouchability, despite the fact that he is a Mahar and hence considered untouchable. According to Pramod Nayar, 'Bhimayana radicalises the form of the comic book as well as the genre of the biography' (3). The text has the capacity to re-historicise Indian history by writing from the margins since it makes use of narrative methods such as dialogues, written statements, thoughts, newspaper clippings and headlines. The story of *Bhimayana* is divided into three sections: 'Water', 'Shelter' and 'Travel'. The first section of the story is meant to reflect the struggle of Dalits, who are prevented from gaining access to water supplies. It mentions an incident from when Ambedkar was a student and the peon at his school did not permit him to drink water. The section 'Shelter' examines the concept of 'home', which Ambedkar did not have access to because of his Dalit status. The final part, 'Travel', shows how a person's caste might prevent them from travelling anywhere, even on a bus. When expressing the plight of the Dalits, graphic artists have also incorporated the methods of reportage and journalism into their work.

DALIT AUTOBIOGRAPHIES

Autobiography turned out to be a very powerful mode of self-assertion as well as self-construction among Dalits in India since 1960 with the publication of the first self narrative in Marathi *Balutha Social Claim* (1978) by Daya Pawar and subsequently in various other languages such as Hindi, Malayalam, Telugu, Tamil, Kannada, Gujarati, Punjabi, etc. As a matter of fact, these autobiographical interventions gave expressions to the agony and deprivation of a group of people who faced caste exploitation and such narratives showed dissent and protest against all power structures which targeted them socially, politically, economically and culturally. Apart from being a narrative of an individual self, Dalit autobiographics construct a collective identity and a collective self in the sense that the trials and tribulations of an entire marginalised community are inscribed for social justice. We have such powerful life-texts such as Barna's *Karukku* (1992), Omprakash Valmiki's *Joothan* (1997), Arvinda Malagathi's *Government Brahmana*, Siddalingaya's *Ooru Keri*, Ramayya's *Ma Neyara* and Govindareya's *Manavilled a Varamadhye* and Laxman Gaikwad's *Uchalya*. Dalit autobiography is the most powerful genre after Dalit poetry in inscribing resistance and anger of a group of people who have been victimised by upper class groups in India.

SHORT TAKES

Women's Life Narratives in India

Autobiography as a mode of expression gives voice to women and allows them to reveal their inner world without any inhibitions from a male-centred social structure. Such narratives question the institution of marriage, unveiling all sorts of discrimination and exploitation encountered by women in a patriarchal society. Writing gives much-needed agency to women, and it is an act of liberation in their self-revelation. However, such autobiographies differ based on their social status. Carolyn G. Heilbrun in *Writing a Women's Life* introduces the four ways in which a woman's life can be narrated: '... the women herself may tell it, in what she chooses to call an autobiography; she may tell it in what she chooses to call fiction; a biographer, woman or man, may write a biography, or the woman may write her own life in advance of living it, unconsciously and without realizing or naming the process' (102). Autobiographies by women such as Amrita Pritam (*The Revenue Stamp*), Kamala Das (*My Story*), Shobhaa De (*Selective Memory*), Dalip Kaur Tiwana, Sharanjeet Shan, Mrinal Pande, Benazir Bhutto and Bangladeshi writer Taslima Nasrin are very blunt in the expression of their innermost feelings. Showing fidelity and truth, they vehemently target social taboos and prevalent customs. Women's autobiographies generally highlight the emotional side of their life while discussing their relations with parents, husbands, and other relatives. In fact, the subjects occupy different positions in the narrative space, that is, the external or social self, namely, their social relations, the private self, the psychological experiences of subjects, and the familial self, which is bound to parents, children, and others.

In the context of women's writing in India, the two-volume project, *Women Writing in India* (1991) edited by Susie Tharu and K. Lalita, proved to be a praiseworthy and pioneering effort in resurrecting many writings by women who were forced to live in obscurity due to patriarchy and other power structures. However, these anthologies have only included writings by women in twelve Indian languages and English, leaving out Punjabi, Rajasthani, Assamese and other languages. Apart from locating rare texts, the initiative deconstructs the Western canon and its paternalistic emphasis on so-called universal principles that are intended to apply to all women. Most significantly, they have these authors' and their writings' contexts, delving into mechanisms such as patriarchy, race and colonialism. According to Chanda, the anthology by Tharu and Lalita is an attempt to develop an aesthetic and create a context in which women's writing can be read 'not as new monuments to existing institutions and cultures... but as documents' displaying the politics of (female) Self formation 'at the margins of patriarchies reconstituted by the emerging bourgeoisies of empire and nation' (36). The two volumes, in fact, focus on women's quest for selfhood and trace a long tradition of such narratives in the form of songs, poems, auto/biographies, memoirs, letters, and so on, beginning in the sixth century BC with the Pali *Therigatha* and continuing through Bhakti poetry of the medieval period represented by Kannada poets Akkamahadevi and Sule Sankawa. The inclusion or rather discovery of certain letters, memoirs and speeches, particularly the autobiographies of Rassundari Devi (Bengali), Ramabai Ranade (Marathi), Binodini Dasi (Bengali), Cornelia Sorabji (English) and Lakshmibai Tilak (Marathi), form a crucial component of the project.

IMAGINING NATION

Political auto/biographies narrate a nation as they link 'personhood to nationhood as aspects of the same cultural and historical situation' (Wagner-Egelhaaf 228). The autobiographical subject, like a nation, is linked to 'a specific place, with its political culture, its history and very often unsettled population' (228). Every autobiography provides a discursive space in which facts and fiction coexist, and the process of self-making is a never-ending process of myth-making in which the autobiographer attempts to construct a culturally or nationally rooted version of the subject. The life narrative attempts to create a fictitious unity and coherence to a person's life by choosing or omitting specific events when plotting a life. Therefore, there are bound to be gaps and silences in life texts, and a single version is practically not possible. As Françoise Lionnet has written: 'If the field of autobiographical studies has taught us anything for the past 20 years, it is that self and community, identity and nation, are such complex webs of feelings and desires that there is no simple formula for understanding the dynamics of subjectivity and identification' (Wagner-Egelhaaf 379).

Many forms of life writing, like autobiography, biography, diary, etc., were introduced by colonisers in colonies as a project of colonial modernity, and after achieving independence, most of these forms became acts or practices of empowering the erstwhile colonies in the construction of their national identities. Hence, we can see that life writing has been a crucial component of postcolonial writing. Autobiographies of the so-called great and famous have a wider dimension, and they can be considered biographies of a nation because a nation is narratively constructed through the perspective of a writer. Thus, Gandhi's autobiography can be considered the biography of modern India because his life is intertwined with so many modern Indian events.

Life stories of subjects who are regionally important inscribe subnational or regional identities, and we have the life histories of leaders of Dravidian movement in Tamil Nadu as very good examples. The dominant trope of Dalit life narratives, according to Udaya Kumar is 'the insistent appearance of humiliation' (17). He adds: 'By recounting experiences of humiliation, Dalit autobiographies make a public claim regarding the norms that govern the treatment of each other in society' (17). Dalit autobiographies play an important role in the reconstruction of Dalit cultural historiography in the postcolonial context. According to Raj Kumar, 'writing autobiography is a political act because there is an assertion of the narrative self' (3). He further writes, 'on the face of several oppressive forces, these authors with their growing perceptions, and mature imagination, capture the tensions, which grow out of a continuous battle between "loss of identity", and "asserting of self"' (150).

I AM MALALA

In her autobiography, *I am Malala: The Story of the Girl Who Stood Up for Education and was shot by the Taliban* (2013), Malala Yousafzai narrates her evolution from a girl in the Swat valley who experienced oppression into an activist for the rights of women across the globe. The life writing describes the political atmosphere of Pakistan, and addresses issues such as the deprivation of education and the need to reform religious orthodoxy. Malala gives details about the life of her mother, who was bound to domestic duties of cooking, cleaning and bringing up children. In fact, we get exhaustive details regarding the cultural practices of Swat valley, especially the negative influence of patriarchy on women. She has been bold enough to openly challenge the Taliban, even after she was shot in the head in 2012 by religious fanatics. She is courageous enough to observe: 'I am Malala. My world has changed but I have not.' The text inspires readers as a powerful motivational narrative, and the indefatigable spirit of the subject was honoured when she was awarded the Nobel Prize for Peace in 2014.

REFERENCES

Anderson, Linda. *Autobiography*. Routledge, 2001.

Arnold, David, and Stuart Blackburn. *Telling Lives in India: Biography, Autobiography and Life History*. Permanent Black, 2004.

Ashcroft, Bill, Gareth Griffiths, and Helen Tiffin. *The Empire Writes Back: Theory and Practice in Post-colonial Literatures*. Routledge, 1989.

Bergland, Betty Ann. "National Identity and Life Writing." *Encyclopedia of Life Writing: Autobiographical and Biographical Forms Volume 2*, edited by Margaretta Jolly. Fitzroy Dearborn Publishers, 2001.

Chakrabarty, Dipesh. *Provincialising Europe: Postcolonial Thought and Historical Difference*. Princeton UP, 2000.

Chakraborty, Suryendu. "Unpacking caste politics through the multimodal communicative landscape of *Bhimayana: Experiences of Untouchability*." *Rupkatha Journal on Interdisciplinary Studies in Humanities*, vol. 12, no. 4, July-September, 2020, pp. 1–8.

Chanda, Swati. *"Women Writing in India: 600 B.C. to the Present* (review)." *MFS Modern Fiction Studies*, vol. 39, no. 1, Spring 1993, pp. 211–14.

Devy, G. N. "Romantic, Post-Romantic and Neo-Romantic Autobiography in Indian English Literature." *Autobiographical and Biographical Writing in the Commonwealth*, edited by Doireann MacDermott. Editorial AUSA, 1984, pp. 63–67.

Dirks, N. B. *Castes of Mind: Colonialism and the Making of Modern India*. Princeton UP, 2001.

Evans, Mary. *Missing Persons: The Impossibility of Auto/biography*. Routledge, 1999.

Felman, Shoshana, and Dori Laub. *Testimony: Crises of Witnessing in Literature, Psychoanalysis, and History*. Routledge, 1992.

Gunn, Janet V. "A Politics of Experience: Leila Khaled's My People Shall Live: The Autobiography of a Revolutionary." *De/Colonizing the Subject: The Politics of Gender in Women's Autobiography*, edited by Sidonie Smith and Julia Watson. U of Minnesota P, 1992.

Heilbrun, Carolyn G. *Writing a Woman's Life*. Norton,1988.

Hornung, Alfred, and Ernstpeter Ruhe, editors. "Preface." *Postcolonialism and Autobiography: Michelle Cliff, David Dabydeen, Opal Palmer Adisa*. Rodopi, p. 3.

Huddart, David. *Postcolonial Theory and Autobiography*. Routledge, 2008.

Jolly, Margaretta, editor. *Encyclopedia of Life Writing: Autobiographical and Biographical Forms Volume 1*. Fitzroy Dearborn Publishers, 2001.

Kim, Lee-Von. "Scenes of Af/filiation: Family Photographs in Postcolonial Life Writing." *Life Writing*, vol. 12, no. 4, 2015, pp. 401–15, doi: 10.1080/14484528.2015.1086874.

Kumar, Raj. *Dalit Personal Narratives: Reading Caste, Nation and Identity*. Orient Blackswan, 2011.

Kumar, Udaya. *Writing the First Person: Literature, History, and Autobiography in Modern Kerala*. Permanent Black, 2016.

Lebdai, Benaouda. *Autobiography as a Writing Strategy in Postcolonial Literature*. Cambridge Scholars Publishing, 2015.

Lionnet, Françoise. "A Politics of the 'We'?: Autobiography, Race and Nation." *American Literary History*, vol. 13, no. 2, 2001, pp. 376–92.

Malti-Douglas, Fedwa. *Men, Women and God(s): Nawal El Saadawi and Arab Feminist Poetics*. U of California P, 1995.

Moore-Gilbert, Bart. *Postcolonial Life - Writing: Culture, Politics and Self-representation*. Routledge, 2009.

Nayar, Pramod. "Towards a postcolonial critical literacy: *Bhimayana* and the Indian graphic novel." *Studies in South Asian Film and Media*, vol. 3, no. 1, 2011, pp. 1–21.

Ramaswamy, Vijaya, and Yogesh Sharma. *Biography as History: Indian Perspectives*. Orient Blackswan, 2009.

Rushdie, Salman. *Midnight's Children*. Penguin, 1980.

Said, Edward. *Out of Place: A Memoir*. Granta, 1999.

Smith, Sidonie, and Julia Watson. *Reading Autobiography: A Guide for Interpreting Life Narratives*. U of Minnesota P, 2001.

Srinivasan, Maria Preethi. "Constructing Aboriginal and Dalit Women's Subjectivity and Making 'Difference' Speak: An Illustration through the Writings of Jackie Huggins, Kumud Pawde and Bama." *Southerly*, vol. 70, no. 3, 2012, pp. 95–15.

Torchin, Leshu. *Creating the Witness: Documenting Genocide on Film, Video, and the Internet*. U of Minnesota P, 2012.

Vijayasree, C. "Indian Biography in English." *Indian Journal of American Studies*, vol. 27, no. 2, 1997, pp. 11–14.

Wagner-Egelhaaf, Martina, editor. *Handbook of Autobiography/Autofiction*. De Gruyter, 2017.

Whitlock, Gillian. *Postcolonial Life Narratives: Testimonial Transactions*. Oxford UP, 2015.

Non-literary Forms of Self Narration

BIOPICS AND DOCUMENTARIES

Biopics are biographical movies that tell the stories of historical figures or famous people based on key moments in their lives. The incidents that are narrated in a biopic reflect the director's politics, but at the same time, the selection of events is also unavoidable. There are biopics centred on both men and women; the former are typically hagiographical, focusing on their characters' heroic deeds, whereas the latter focus on female victimisation. Biopics are hard for actors playing the lead roles, and Ben Kingsley as Mahatma Gandhi in *Gandhi* (1982), Robert Downey Jr. as Charlie Chaplin in *Chaplin* (1992) and Eddie Redmayne as Stephen Hawking in *The Theory of Everything* (2014) are no exception. It is worth mentioning that biographical filmic stories function as memory archives where the past is reactivated. Autobiopics are a sub-genre of biopics in which the subjects of the films portray themselves. *The Jackie Robinson Story* (1950), *The Greatest* (1977) with Muhammad Ali and *Private Parts* (1977) with Howard Stern are all good examples.

A biopic is a cultural tool because it shows one way to look at a famous person and, in doing so, imprints a particular image of the hero in the public's mind (Sheldon 1). He adds: 'They can introduce interesting, important people, or events in history to new audiences, but can also distort real life events in a controversial manner that does a disservice to the life of the figure depicted' (1). Thus, we can see that 'the activity of meaning-making is inherently funneled through the ideologies of the elite' (1).

Biopics are hagiographic in nature, with the protagonists representing a nation and evoking a sense of collective identity (Nayar 604). According to Murray Pomerance,

> We participate to some degree in the experiences and events by virtue of which some other person has apparently become notable. We explore the notability that lingers in the story as a kind of shadow trace that follows the subject. The biopic subject is at once notable in objective terms, having become what he is; and notable dramaturgically, since the adoration of crowds is an ostensible component of the subject's story as recounted on the screen. (30)

A biopic constructs a subject as a 'national symbolic' (Berlant 155) who embodies a nation by appealing to masses: 'the collective possession of its official texts – the flag, Uncle Sam, Mount Rushmore, the Pledge of Allegiance, even now, perhaps, JFK and Dr Martin Luther King – creates a national "public" that constantly repudiates political knowledge where it exceeds performatively mythic national codes' (Berlant 155 qtd. in Nayar 606). Because the true story of a biopic is already known to the audience, there is little suspense and no need for the audience to stretch their imaginations. As Pomerance observes:

> With the biopic subject in mind, the viewer does not have to stretch the imagination, as in standard fiction film, in order to find some bridging that allows for the transfer of the subject's putative experience as his own; the biopic, after all, takes place in the world space of the viewer's own life and experience. Even if removed by glory, power, or fame, the subject is always also a person one could have touched. (28)

The biopic's subject is interesting both because of who the subject is and how their story is told onscreen, because of what they have become and because of how their story is told. Social importance is a less vital aspect of the subject's 'life' (30) than fame.

SHORT TAKES

GANDHI

Richard Attenborough's biopic *Gandhi* (1982) has played a pioneering role in constructing an iconic image of Gandhi and popularising the Gandhi legend in the West. It is interesting to note that no biopic on Gandhi was attempted by anyone before 1980, when a film maker from the West appeared on the scene. Obviously, he got the full support of the government of India. In fact, Gandhi was based on Louis Fischer's biography, *The Life of Mahatma Gandhi* and though we do not see anything about Gandhi's childhood and youth, 'there is a deliberate attempt at iconizing him, this being helped by the acts of Ben Kingsley's remarkable interpretation...' (Markovits 28). We may notice that the biopic has failed to explore Gandhi's inner life and seems to sentimentalise situations by telescoping the image of Gandhi by sidelining other important characters such as Ambedkar. Attenborough's *Gandhi* ends with Gandhi's march towards triumph and martyrdom, and it is used as an instrument in promoting the state ideology.

DIGITAL LIFE NARRATIVES

Aside from the usual navigators, like teens and young adults, the older generation has a lot to gain from digital space as well. They form online communities to share their stories through journals, weblogs and other means. The 'I' in cyberspace is multiple and hybridised, and while studying online life writings, we may contend that virtual space is confronted with the traces of the self. Here, Judith Butler's notion of 'substitution' is important because 'I' is understood only in connection with the other. In "Violence, Mourning, Politics", Butler writes, 'I am not fully known to myself, because part of what I am is the enigmatic traces of others' (46). She observes:

> This failure to narrate fully may well indicate how we are, from the start, ethically implicated in the lives of others. . . . [T]he way we are, from the start, interrupted by alterity may render us incapable of offering narrative closure for our lives. . . . [O]ur "incoherence" establishes the way in which we are constituted in relationality: implicated, beholden, derived,

sustained by a social world that is beyond us and before us. (*Giving an Account* 64)

In studying online life narratives, the aspect of relationality is a key factor because 'Self-representation has everything to do with others, and one's personal material, from printed memoir to web post, is never completely one's own' (Pulda 183). However, 'The sites of online life writing are living documents, subject to revision, erasure, and vandalism' (192).

Ethics of Life Writing Online

As John Zuern writes in *Biography's* first *Online Lives* issue: 'Attention to material contexts helps us see that many producers of online writing are not simply "using" available channels of communication, but are actively making connections: building virtual homes, bridges, and hybrid public-private spaces that transform cultural landscapes on and beyond the Internet' (xiv). An important aspect of digital lives is that they offer space for 'disadvantaged voices' dissemination on the web' (Pulda 194).

Autobiography exists in different media forms and other 'unlikely documents' (Kadar 2) such as 'a deportation list, an art exhibit, reality TV, Internet websites and chat rooms, memos and propaganda documents, memories – as well as familiar literary genres, such as the play, the long poem, the short story' (2). Unlike the conventional forms of life writing, what makes digital life unique is 'their ability to produce the image of an identifiable person, figure or avatar' (Jolly 557). In fact, they are 'performed via personal websites, weblogs and social networking sites, and are located somewhere between traditional autobiographical poetics and the new possibilities offered by information technology' (557).

Traditionally, autobiography is considered to be the story of a real person, and the text reflects the personality of the autobiographer, but when it comes to the new standard of digital life narratives, we see a paradigm shift, where a real person is replaced by 'computers and algorithms' (558), and we see that '"stories" often become commodities, owned by corporations that provide the means for such life-writing, such as Facebook or Instagram' (558). He continues: 'What the digital age requires are therefore new models

of *genuinely* digital self-construction and genuinely *digital* auto/
biography, able to keep up with technological, social and aesthetic
changes' (558).

Recent technological developments in digital media have forced
us to rethink the traditional meaning of autobiography because
'text' is no longer a deciding factor in an autobiography; other forms
of media, such as photographs, videos and other files, also define
a subject. Thus, one can see an increase in dependence on media
platforms to articulate a self. Second, the rapid advancement of
technology makes it extremely difficult to establish a unified self
with a specific meaning (Jolly 559). The concept of automediality
developed by Dünne and Moser in 2008 can be used as 'a theoretical
framework in studying digital life narratives given the fact that a
pre-existing individual identity is an illusion and that our identity
is constructed by our daily interactions through media platforms'
(559).

Digital life narratives, apart from offering immense possibilities,
also offer certain challenges regarding identity formation; the
question of whether they assert 'existing models of identity or
whether new media invite play with and even subversion of
identities' (Kadar 25) is indeed puzzling. Online life narratives
are 'not solely or even primarily written' (26). 'Digital writing is
also distinctive because of how it is reproduced, transmitted, and
stored. The networked computer environment in which texts such
as personal home pages exist, and through which they are read and
interpreted, impacts both their design and their reception' (26).
People make use of the internet 'to access genealogical information,
to communicate with others to whom they might be related, to gain
information about places, historical events, and figures that shape
their lives, and, of course, to create their self-representations in
word, image, sound, and movement' (26–27). For instance, 'the self
that is represented on a personal home page is not a private self but
a very public one – more public than a self represented in a printed
book because of the (potential) global reach of the audience' (27).

In cyberspace, writing about every life is a possibility, and
anyone who has access to the internet can publish/upload their life
experience without waiting for the publisher's approval. Besides,
online publishing is faster and cheaper. Digital space brings more

authenticity and helps form a connection between author and reader because, on a platform such as a homepage, we come across traces of life including early life, personal achievements, interests, hobbies, genealogical charts, ancestral details, photographs, videos, and other visual texts that bring a sense of relationality and authenticity. However, the reading of such stories is always *technologically mediated* (emphasis added) by gadgets such as mobile phones, tablets, personal computers or laptops, etc. 'Self-representation in social media performs work in the world that is autobiographical, interpersonal, and, increasingly, institutional and public' (Morrison 41).

The self that is represented in social media life texts is private, but it is more of an interpersonal and public one, though there are individual variations in style, agenda and audience. Such online life texts on YouTube, Twitter, Facebook, Instagram, etc., are multimodal, autobiographical, political and complex with 'aural, textual, pictorial, photographic' (41) combinations. However, their authorship is 'attuned to technical, social, and generic exigencies as much as to simply literary or creative ones' (42). Interpreting such texts requires interdisciplinary approaches ranging from close reading, rhetorical genre theory to new media/ digital humanities approaches.

Because of what Julie Rak calls 'the digital turn' (164), the already large field of autobiography studies has grown even more, and we now have completely new ways of presenting ourselves online, like online obituary narratives. Cyberspace is now a forum for memorialising the dead, and it is a democratic one, too, because ordinary people are mourned online as well. MuchLoved.Com, GoneTooSoon.org, Legacy.com and In Memory Of. are just a few of the many memorial sites that might reach a larger audience.

Our memories are personal, and we remember them in the present through images. Things like religion and the law also shape them. No wonder our reconstructions of the past have personal agendas filtered by our thoughts, hopes, emotions, fears, etc. Therefore, we may remember it as a political act. It is important to remember that our memories in digital space are stored and circulated as visual images, but unfortunately, such images are inherently prone to editing and manipulation and are therefore highly unreliable. Sonia Wilson stresses that 'our sense of self is bound up with acts of seeing' and that 'our relations both to ourselves and to others are visually constituted' (448). In order to be cautious about it, Eleanor Ty argues that we need to 'read between and behind the images, paying sharper attention to the social, political, historical structures and situations in which these pictures and subsequent memories were forged' (365).

Reality television is another recent mode of self articulation through television media, and there are popular shows like *Big Brother, Survivor, The Amazing Race, Joe Millionaire, Paradise Hotel* and *Temptation Island*. It may be argued that 'this representation of reality depends on the auto/biographical performances of the shows' participants' (Kadar 45).

Scholars, particularly Ana Belén Martínez García, argue that online TED Talks by activists addressing a larger audience on specific personal experiences, evoking empathy, can be classified as life writing. In fact, they intersect the two fields, that is, life writing and human rights, and have an ethical and emancipatory angle too. TED talks give activists a new way to talk about themselves online and help shape who they are as people. Thus, digital platforms pave the way for online activism, generating a sense of 'narrative empathy' (Keen 3).

The conventional narrative about the global collapse of indigenous peoples' cultures often refers to them as 'people of the past', but can social media actually provide them with more power in the digital age? Bronwyn Carlson and Ryan Frazer in *Indigenous Digital Life: The Practice and Politics of Being Indigenous on Social Media* (2021) argue that social media acts as 'a space of Indigenous action, production, and creativity; we see Indigenous social media users as powerful agents, who interact with and shape their immediate worlds with skill, fair and nous; and instead of being "a people of the past," we show that Indigenous digital life is often *future-orientated*, working towards building better relations, communities and worlds' (vii).

RITUALS AND PERFORMANCES

Autobiographical enactments are also possible through dance performances where a subject's self is constructed through bodily movements in front of the audience. Usually, such self-presentations take place through solo presentations, and we have Isadora Duncan as a good example where 'authorship (choreography), presentation (dance performance) and outline configuration (self-management) are generally combined in one person' (Jolly 544). Here, the body becomes a text and a spectacle where discourses are generated.

Autobiographical theatre opens up a new possibility to experiment with different shades of one's identity. It problematises how our subjectivity is produced via performance. Here, it is significant to take the poststructuralist stance of a fragmentary subject with multiple dimensions. A performer can 'play' their role, giving multiple versions to 'subvert the autobiographical coherence of the self, thereby resisting the white, bourgeois norm of individualism expressed in autobiographical narrative' (Smith 31).

MONUMENTS AND MEMORIALS

Statues of great personalities who have made significant contributions to various civilisations are frequently erected, and constructing monuments to them is comparable to their influence over people through the values they championed. It can also be considered a show of respect and gratitude for their invaluable and everlasting contributions. In India, we see monuments to Mahatma Gandhi, Bhimrao Ambedkar, Swami Vivekananda and others solemnly placed in public locations and available to the public gaze; they are installed in 'a space wherein individuals can become public beings' (Kendall 4). But, it might be true to say that these physical signs of life make people think about a number of ideas related to the legendary figures. The fact that they have been around for a long time and still have meaning shows that the ideas they stood for will always be important. Statues of many different people are put up everywhere, but it is important to keep politics in mind when choosing whose statues are to be installed. The approval of the state and other institutions of power appears to be required when installing monuments at various sites and exposing them to public inspection. Throughout India, there are sculptures of historical personalities that serve as texts, describing unique periods of Indian history and therefore contributing to national/ regional historiography. Similarly, the creation of hero sculptures contributes to national iconography.

On the other hand, some people who have made significant contributions to their country have been deliberately obscured by vested interests and are hardly documented in official histories, while statues of divine beings and spiritual/religious subjects can be found all around the country. Clearly, such religious state apparatuses result in the formation of a so-called 'religious public sphere'. Saints' statues are moral edifices and ethical indoctrination structures; they silently propagate certain beliefs and norms.

'Commemorative ceremonies and bodily practices' (Connerton 7) are among the various ways in which various societies remember their citizens and their accomplishments, and such acts lead to the formation of what is known as social memory, which is 'best termed the activity of historical reconstruction' (7). Social memory is founded on the idea that memory is socially formed, notably through social groupings like 'kinship, religion, and class affiliations that individuals are able to acquire, to localize, and recall their memories' (36). 'Grandparents' tales, family histories, biographies, autobiographies, commemoration rituals and other ritual acts are some of the ways these social groups carry on their collective memories over generations' (38). We could say that putting up statues and monuments is also a way to build social memories and remember the past.

Statues hold memories, and they are built to remember a historical event or to honour the great things that a person has done. While looking at the statues, contemporary society can learn a lot. 'Visual representations like statues are used as apparatuses to disseminate the ideology of governments, and thus they become the paragons of dominant discourse' (Nair and Jose 241). The statues of Mahatma Gandhi are a good example here.

A FEW OTHER NON-LITERARY FORMS

Life writing is an ever-expanding field of study, and there are many forms, such as oral narratives, petitions, testimonies, church registers and court testimonies, that are worth exploring. As a material mode of life writing, an epitaph is a means of self-assertion, of commemorating the dead, by passing on a person's contribution to posterity with epigrammatic brevity. Crystalised in poetry or prose, an epitaph appears on a tombstone or mortuary monument. 'It is the public concern that is paramount, as these monuments allow a single individual to live on in the collective memory of the group due to their meritorious life as shaped in the form of exemplary biography or mediated through iconographic programs' (Jolly 579). Interestingly, there is research that centres on 'the notion of autobiography as an epitaph or monument to a past life, based on the "fiction of a voice-from-beyond-the grave"' (de Man 77). 'The use of the tomb as a site for self-presentation shows the close link between funerary cult, history/continuation and literature' (Assmann 66). Epitaphs differ in style and content, as they range from 'the simple mention of the name and dates of birth and death (a sort of minimal biography) to detailed eulogies and express contemporary ideas about the relationship between life and death, individual and social identity, as well as the rhetoric tradition' (Jolly 580). They aim to perpetuate the memory of the deceased. However, we may also look at the narcissistic aspect of an epitaph, with a person trying to immortalise their deeds for the present and future generations.

A self-portrait is a visual medium of self-representation through forms such as photography, painting, sculpture, video-clips, performative practices, etc. It is 'linked to the concepts of self-consciousness, documentation and identity, self-portraiture follows an intellectual course similar to self-writing practices being at once a claim to and an expression of artistic self-projection' (663).

Different cultures have different ways of telling oral autobiographies, and we can see the author/performer sharing their experiences with the audience, who sometimes joins in. Kathaprasangam in Kerala, Harikatha in Karnataka and a few other states, are good examples of indigenous oral life narratives. The chief characteristics of such forms are 'fragmentation, repetition, metaphorical density and a focus on social relations between the speaking individual and the collectives he/she refers to' (640). However, such oral forms 'raise difficult questions about authorship, authority and agency, the idea that all autobiographical forms, whether oral or written are to some extent collaborative, has been developed in audience oriented research' (645). When art depicts the lives of people close to the subject or is a self-portrait of the subject, it becomes autobiographical. We have autobiographical paintings such as Rubens' *Self-Portrait with Helena Fourment and Clara Johanna* and Rembrandt's *Self-Portrait in a Tavern* as good examples.

REFERENCES

Assmann, Jan. "Schrift, Tod und Identität. Das Grab als Vorschule der Literatur im alten Ägypten." *Schrift und Gedächtnis*, edited by Aleida Assmann, Jan Assmann and Christof Hardmeier. Fink, 1983, pp.64–93.

Berlant, Lauren. "America, 'Fat,' the Fetus." *boundary* 2, vol. 21, no. 3, 1994, pp. 145–95.

Butler, Judith. "Violence, Mourning, Politics." *Precarious Life: The Powers of Mourning and Violence*. Verso, 2006, pp.19–49.

---. *Giving an Account of Oneself*. Fordham UP, 2005.

Carlson, Bronwyn and Ryan Frazer. *Indigenous Digital Life The Practice and Politics of Being Indigenous on Social Media*. Palgrave Macmillan, 2021.

Connerton, Paul. *How Societies Remember*. Cambridge UP, 1989.

de Man, Paul. "Autobiography as De-Facement." *The Rhetoric of Romanticism*. Columbia UP, 1984, pp.67–82.

Jolly, Margaretta, editor. *Encyclopedia of Life Writing: Autobiographical and Biographical Forms Volume 2*. Fitzroy Dearborn Publishers, 2001.

Kadar, Marlene, editor. *Tracing the Autobiographical*, edited by Marlene Kadar, Linda Warley, Jeanne Perreault and Susanna Egan. Wilfrid Laurier UP, 2005.

Keen, Suzanne. "Strategic Empathizing: Techniques of Bounded, Ambassadorial, and Broadcast Narrative Empathy." *Deutsche Vierteljahrsschrift für Literaturwissenchaft und Geistesgeschichte*, vol. 82, no. 3, 2008, pp. 477–93.

Kendall, Paul Murray. *The Art of Biography*. W. W. Norton & Co Inc, 1985.

Markovits, Claude. *The Un-Gandhian Gandhi: The Life and Afterlife of the Mahatma*. Permanent Black, 2004.

Morrison, Aimee. "Social, Media, Life Writing: Online Lives at Scale, Up Close, and In Context." *Research Methodologies for Auto/biography Studies*, edited by Kate Douglas and Ashley Barnwell. Routledge, 2019.

Nair, Rajesh V. and Philip Jose. "Sculpting Lives: A Reading of the Life Narration of Adi Sankara at Kalady." *Samyukta*, vol. XII, no. 2, July 2012, pp. 241–49.

Nayar, Pramod K. "Biopics: The Year in India." *Biography*, vol. 40, no. 4, Fall 2017, pp. 604–10.

Pomerance, Murray. "Empty Words: Houdini and Houdini." *Invented Lives, Imagined Communities: The Biopic and American National Identity*, edited by William H. Epstein and R. Barton Palmer. SUNY P, 2016, pp. 25–48.

Pulda, Molly. "Victim/Victor: Stalking the Subject of Online Life Writing." *Biography*, vol. 38, no. 2, Spring 2015, pp. 181–204.

Rak, Julie. "Derailment: Going Offline to Be Online." *a/b: Auto/ Biography Studies*, vol. 32, no. 2, 2017, pp. 163–65. https://doi.org/10.1080/08989575.2017. 1287863

Sheldon, Zachary. "Public memory and popular culture: biopics, #MeToo, and David Foster Wallace." *Atlantic Journal of Communication*, doi: 10.1080/15456870.2020.1712603

Smith, Sidonie. "Performativity, Autobiographical Practice, Resistance." *Auto/Biography studies*, vol. 10, no. 1, 2009, pp.17–33.

Ty, Eleanor. "Memory, Digital Media, and Life Writing." *Auto/Biography studies*, vol. 32, no. 2, 2017, pp. 363–65.

Wilson, Sonia. "Show and Tell: Negotiating Self and Seeing in *Les Photos d'Alix* by Jean Eustache." *Life Writing*, vol. 12, no. 4, 2015, pp. 447–63.

Zuern, John. "Online Lives: Introduction." *Online Lives*. Spec. issue of *Biography*, vol. 26, no. 1, Winter 2003, pp. v–xxv.

Chapter Six

Life Writing and Genders

U nlike women's life histories, which address 'the issues of femininity and femaleness' (Morgan 35), life narratives by men discuss 'fatherhood, sexuality and violence' (35). Autobiography is considered a masculine genre (Brodzki and Schenck 1) and traditional auto/biographies inscribe male success stories and project individualist notions of self. It is only recently that male life writers have turned to the aspect of masculinity (Jolly, Volume 1, 360), and we have some recent examples such as Philip Roth's *Patrimony* (1991), Brian Keenan's prison memoir *An Evil Cradling* (1993) and Blake Morrison's *And When Did You Last See Your Father?* (1993). In *Food and Masculinity in Contemporary Autobiographies* (2018), Pascual Soler examines how food becomes a very important narrative trope in men's autobiographies. While debating the role of gender in life writing, perhaps, we need to give prominence to the life narratives of women and other sexual minorities.

WOMEN AND LIFE WRITING

Women's life writing includes a variety of genres and sub-genres such as autobiography, biography, diaries, journals, letters, testimonies, blogs and so on, and they all contribute to the construction of female subjectivity through writing. In the past, women's autobiographies were not included in the traditional canon, and life narratives by men were placed on the centre stage. The self narratives of Saint Augustine and Rousseau were foregrounded. But of late, the form of autobiography has been one of the most important sites of feminist debate precisely because it demonstrates that there are many different ways of writing about the subject. The turn to autobiographical texts within feminism, therefore, also enabled critics to replay the problem of the subject in ways that are often experimental, which seemed to lie outside the terms of theory as it was then thought (Anderson 87). When it comes to African American autobiographies, they might be seen as autoethnographies, as they represent a whole group of people; hence, such works embody a collective identity. As a result, these works can be considered emancipatory. Barbara Johnson points out the problem of a woman's autobiographer in *A World of Difference*: 'The problem for the female autobiographer is, on the one hand, to resist the pressure of masculine autobiography as the only literary genre available for her enterprise, and, on the other, to describe a difficulty in conforming to a female ideal which is largely a fantasy of the masculine, not the feminine, imagination' (154). However, since 1980, there has been a paradigm shift: '(T)he self-discovery of female identity appears to acknowledge the real presence and recognition of another consciousness, and the disclosure of female self is linked to the identification of some "other"' (210).

As a genre, women's autobiography has come of age since the 1980s with the introduction of feminist, postcolonial and postmodern strategies of approaching subjectivity. The unified, solitary self has been replaced by the fragmented self. As a matter of fact, 'the texts and theory of women's autobiography have been pivotal for revising our concepts of women's life issues: growing up female, coming to voice, affiliation, sexuality and textuality, the life cycle' (Smith and Watson 5).

Female Pedagogy

Autobiographies written by women emphasise 'positive images of women' (7). These texts challenge patriarchal norms and empower women by allowing them to express their experiences via writing. Women's writings, including autobiographies, have now become a part of courses at college and university levels. Sidonie Smith shows the double-voiced structure of women's autobiographies, 'as it reveals the tensions between their desire for narrative authority and their concern about excessive self-exposure' (12). In their work, *Life/Lines: Theorizing Women's Autobiography,* Brodzki and Schenck expand the scope of women's autobiographical textuality to films, painted self-portraits and poetry (12). Several seminal works published after 1980 bolstered the field of women's autobiography studies, including Smith and Watson's *De/Colonizing the Subject: The Politics of Gender in Women's Autobiography* (1992), Francoise Lionnet and Ronnie Scharfman's *Post/Colonial Conditions: Exiles, Migrations, and Nomadisms* (1993), Lionnet's *Postcolonial Representations* (1995) and Barbara Harlow's *Resistance Literature* (1987).

Women's Autobiography and Canon

While tracing the history of women's autobiography, we encounter distinct instances of gender discrimination. So-called 'great' or 'exemplary' subjects were textualised, and those chosen for public display were men from affluent social classes. Autobiographies are typically written about individuals who, through their triumphs, have the potential to affect their society through their individuality. Speaking on the relative scarcity of women's autobiographies, Valerie Sanders observes: 'The difficulty of attributing "meaning" to a life that has appeared random, private, passive, and incoherent has been a major stumbling-block in the evolution of a women's tradition of autobiography' (Jolly, Volume 2, 946). While early autobiographies by women such as Margery Kempe documented spiritual experiences, the form gained secular credentials later, and we have autobiographers such as Alice Thornton, Lucy Hutchinson, Margaret Oliphant, Mary Russell Mitford, Elizabeth Missing Sewell, Emmeline Pankhurst, Virginia Woolf, Gertrude Stein, Simone de Beauvoir and Maya Angelou as excellent examples. Women's autobiographies are now an important canon in Life Writing Studies, and they have become 'more sensationalized, more open, and more overtly tragic, with few autobiographers now hesitating to share their griefs with the public' (Sanders 948). There are also female theoreticians of autobiography such as Sidonie Smith,

Bella Brodzki, Celeste Schenk, Regenia Gagnier, Linda Peterson, Mitzi Myers, Liz Stanley, Trev Broughton and Mary Jean Corbett. Women all around the world have more recently been embracing this practice as a means of self-empowerment.

With the advent of the digital revolution, cyber-diaries have also become one of the new forms for women to inscribe their identities, and we can observe a reconfiguration of 'notions of the public and the private: the diarists clearly have an audience but can remain anonymous themselves and even lie about their identities' (Jolly, Volume 2, 952). However, the materiality of the cyber-diary has transformed as it can now be readily deleted online. Apart from providing a space for women to etch their identities through diaries, other digital modalities such as YouTube and social networking sites have empowered them to express dissent and protest against all forms of oppression and exploitation.

Women Biographies/ as Biographers

The development of women's biographies on female subjects is an integral part of the corpus of life writing, and the effect of feminist discussions has resulted in the development of such writings across continents. Collective biographies of women were prevalent in England during the eighteenth century and were produced by writers such as Elizabeth Benger, Mary Robinson (under the pseudonym of Anne Frances Randall), Mary Hays, Matilda Betham, Mary Pilkington and Lucy Aikin. We have the earliest of these collective biographies, Ann Thicknesse's *Sketches of the Lives and Writings of the Ladies of France*, published in 1780. Later, women who made significant contributions to various realms of society were included in anthologies such as national biographies. We have Jessie Carney Smith's *Notable Black American Women* (1992 and 1996), Lynda Anderson's *Notable Women in American History: A Guide to Recommended Biographies and Autobiographies* (1999), and more. While aristocratic ladies and those lauded for their spiritual activities were at first the favoured topics, accomplished women in domains like politics, performance arts and literature subsequently gained attention and were written about. Full-length biographies of specific women were pioneered by Elizabeth Gaskell's testimony to Charlotte Bronte, Margaret Macmillan's *Life of Rachel Macmillan* (1927), Anne Stevenson's study of Plath (*Bitter Fame*, 1990) or Janet Todd's biography of Mary Wollstonecraft (*Mary Wollstonecraft: A Revolutionary Life*, 2000), among others. Sybil Oldfield sums up the evolution of women's biographies in the following manner: 'Women's writing of biography has moved from the spiritual to the intellectual, to the social, and now includes the intimately personal, but there are obvious limitations to any human's total understanding of another...' (950).

Women's Diaries and Journals

A diary is 'an inherently female form' (Jolly, Volume 2, 950), which gives opportunities to women to document their intimate personal experiences. It transgresses the borders between public and private, marking the diary a gendered genre since, in the patriarchal paradigm, the private counts as the realm of the female' (Wagner-Egelhaaf 547). In diaries, 'the borders between fact and fiction are transgressed because the "I" of the diary is subjective and unreliable' (547). According to Susan Rubin Suleiman, the diary is a 'loose form, weaving together a large number of different themes, and stories, that emerge only gradually' (234). The diary is bound by temporal restrictions as it is in the form of daily entries. Paperno defines it as a first-person narrative with the consequence of 'the diary's special relationship to privacy, intimacy, and secrecy' (562). Diaries, like autobiographies, are not only texts but 'practices of shaping and contesting power by establishing agency and the individual "I" in a social and historical context' (Walker 351). Natalie Crouter's *Forbidden Diary: A Record of Wartime Internment 1941–5* (1980), Audre Lorde's experience of breast cancer in *The Cancer Journals* (1980), Augusta de Mist's *Diary of a Journey to the Cape of Good Hope and the Interior of Africa in 1802 and 1803*, Virginia Woolf's *Diary* and Anne Frank's diaries are monumental examples of this genre.

THE DIARY OF ANNE FRANK

The Diary of Anne Frank is one of the most poignant life narratives from a teenage point of view about the horrors of the gruesome Nazi holocaust. Trapped in the Secret Annex attached to Mr Frank's business house, the story details the predicament of Anne and the Frank family, along with a few other people, during World War II. The diary spans over 2 years, starting when Anne was 13 years old, and the readers get to see the pathetic plight of the Jews through her eyes. It is also a coming-of-age life story because the narrator matures and reaches puberty within the secret chamber. The text also highlights the issue of sexuality when Anne develops a passionate relationship with a 16-year-old boy, Peter van Pels, who was also hiding there. Thus, the searing life narrative documents the development of Anne Frank's selfhood from a child to a teenager.

Women's Letters

Letter-writing is a mode of revealing one's identity and women use it as a powerful form. According to Cynthia Huff, 'Some critics have debated whether writing letters traps women within the private domain or whether letter writing can be a political act, precisely in giving women a more subtle form of access to public realms. Both positions focus on the interaction between prescribed gender roles and the act of writing letters' (Jolly, Volume 2, 954). According to Mary A. Favret, 'the letter served as a vehicle for writing women's entry into the political world, because of the letter's democratic tendencies and its ability to translate between the private and public world' (953). Virginia Woolf, Sylvia Plath, Anne Sexton, Isak Dinesen, Vera Brittain and Crystal Eastman are some of the writers who powerfully used the epistolary form.

WRITING OTHER SEXUALITIES

Life writings of marginalised sexualities are 'coming out' narratives whose 'essential plot is self-acceptance through public declaration of one's sexuality' (Jolly, Volume 1, 547). There has been an unprecedented rise in the popularity of the life stories of homosexuals since the 1960s, mainly due to events such as the Gay Liberation Movement of North America, the Stonewall incident in a gay bar in New York in 1969, etc. If early writing by minority sexualities was anonymous, we find subsequent powerful instances of texts such as John Addington Symonds' *Memoirs* (written 1889–90; published posthumously in 1984), Oscar Wilde's *De Profundis* (published posthumously in 1905), Claude Hartland's *The Story of a Life* (1901), Radclyffe Hall's autofiction, *The Well of Loneliness* (1928) and Gertrude Stein's *Autobiography of Alice B. Toklas*. According to Diana Fuss, a gay or lesbian life narrative 'charts transformation, the rejection of an old life for a new one. On the other hand, in revealing a hidden aspect of the self, it asserts continuity with the past' (Jolly, Volume 1, 548). Jolly makes the following observation, defining the larger dimension of gay and lesbian historiography:

> In the "essentialist" view of gay sexuality, the contemporary flourishing of individual life stories represents the new visibility of those previously forced to disguise themselves, to "pass" as heterosexual, a position not so much defended by academics as by autobiographers themselves. In the "constructivist" view, gay sexuality is historical rather than essential or biological in any pure sense. (548)

Recently, writers including David Wojnarowicz, Terenci Moix, Juan Goytisolo, Kathy Acker and William Burroughs have experimented with the form of autobiography by including elements such as irony and parody. As the field of psychoanalysis advanced, we see more texts that explore homosexual personalities, such as George Painter's *Proust* (2 vols., 1959–65) and Leon Edel's *Henry James* (5 vols., 1953–72). A recent development is the flourishing of AIDS narratives in which sexuality as the major concern is replaced by issues such as death, illness and public mourning. Paul Monette's *Becoming a Man: Half a Life Story* (1994) is a notable work representing this trend. Another notable example is *Eight Fought to Live* (2024) by Florence Rosiello.

Hoshang Merchant

Hoshang Merchant is a poet, critic, and autobiographer who is one of India's most notable gay writers. *Yaraana: Gay Writing from India* (1999) is India's first anthology of gay writing. In his autobiography, *The Man Who Would be Queen: Autobiographical Fiction* (2012), Merchant recalls his early familial troubles and the conflicts he encountered as a result of his sexual orientation. Additionally, the author details his sexual activities and how he ends up losing love and affection in his relationships.

It is common knowledge that autobiography as a form of writing lives has been a mode of empowerment for the marginalised. Smith and Watson have underlined that 'deploying autobiographical practices that go against the grain' can constitute 'an "I" that becomes a place of creative and, by implication, political intervention' (qtd. in Anderson 103). Anderson calls autobiography 'the text of the oppressed' (104) and it is 'both a way of testifying to oppression and empowering the subject through their cultural inscription and recognition' (104). However, the politicisation of the subject does not sufficiently address the problem of 'difference' in gender. Stuart Hall argues that discursive practices 'always implicate' the positions from which we speak and therefore 'though we speak, so to say "in our own name", of ourselves and from our own experience, nevertheless who speaks, and the subject who is spoken of, are never identical, never exactly in the same place' (qtd. in Anderson 105).

While debating queer identity, one has to remember that it is fluid, indeterminate and shifting, and this becomes a problematic issue. Paul Gilroy, in his book *The Black Atlantic* (1993) also observes that 'queer is not concerned with definition, fixity or stasis, but is transitive, multiple and anti-assimilationist' (qtd. in Salih 9).

Coming-out Life Narratives

Trans life stories can be categorised as coming-out narratives because they offer challenges to dominant, hegemonic heteronormative discourses. Similarly, Smith comments on narratives about gay men because they 'implicate critiques of enforced social norms of masculinity and might be read more comprehensively within the project of situating male embodiment at a nexus of categories of identity' (Smith and Watson 40). At the same time, there are narratives such as Kathryn Harrison in *The Kiss: A Secret Life* and Michael Ryan in *Secret Life: An Autobiography* that reveal sexuality to such an extent that Smith calls them 'sexual confessions' (40). Smith and Watson observe: 'Coming-out narratives make visible formerly invisible subjects, as gay, bisexual, lesbian, and transgendered subjects inscribe stories of the costs of passing as heteronormative subjects and the liberatory possibilities of legitimation' (108).

SHORT TAKES

REVATHI

A. Revathi's autobiography, *The Truth About Me: A Hijra Life Story* (2010), provides a unique viewpoint on the transgender experience and the numerous ways in which gender relations function, resulting in oppression, subjection, exploitation and marginalisation. For her, claiming an identity means breaking free from the constraints of an unclear identity and given gender and sex roles and establishing personhood in a body and gender of her choosing, a sex that fits her inner self and fundamental identity as a woman. Revathi was born as Doraisamy in the Nammakkal taluk of Tamil Nadu's Salem District.

There is a general perception that life narratives inscribe identities and are narratives of self-assertion. Contrary to this, Smith and Watson argue that 'discursive systems emergent in social structures shape the operations of memory, experience, identity, and embodiment...' (42). In fact, telling personal stories is controlled by certain social strictures before displaying the lives before the reading public. Writing and reading life stories regarding epiphanies or 'turning points' (Cohler 22) experienced in resolving issues of sexual identity fosters an enhanced sense of personal integrity for the writer and in turn an enhanced sense of community for the reader.

REFERENCES

Anderson, Linda. *Autobiography*. Routledge, 2001.

Brodzki, Bella and Celeste Schenck. *Life/Lines: Theorizing Women's Autobiography*. Cornell UP, 1988.

Cohler, Bertram J. *Writing Desire: Sixty Years of Gay Autobiography*. Wisconsin P, 2007.

Johnson, Barbara. "My Monster/My Self." *A World of Difference*. Johns Hopkins UP, 1987.

Jolly, Margaretta, editor. *Encyclopedia of Life Writing: Autobiographical and Biographical Forms Volume 1*. Fitzroy Dearborn Publishers, 2001.

---. *Encyclopedia of Life Writing: Autobiographical and Biographical Forms Volume 2*. Fitzroy Dearborn Publishers, 2001.

Morgan, David. "Masculinity, Autobiography and History." *Gender & History*, vol. 2, no.1, Spring 1990, pp. 34–39.

Oldfield, Sybil. *Collective Biography of Women in Britain, 1550-1900: A Select Annotated Bibliography*. Mansell, 1999.

Paperno, Irina. "What Can Be Done with Diaries?" *The Russian Review*, vol. 63, 2004, pp. 561–73.

Salih, Sarah. *Judith Butler*. Routledge, 2002.

Sanders, Valerie. *The Private Lives of Victorian Women: Autobiography in Nineteenth-Century England*. St Martin's P, 1989.

Smith, Sidonie and Julia Watson. *Women, Autobiography, Theory: A Reader*. The U of Wisconsin P, 1998.

Suleiman, Susan Rubin. "Diary as Narrative: Theory and Practice." *The Search for a New Alphabet. Literary Studies in a Changing World*, edited by Harald Hendrix, Joost Kloek, Sophie Levie and Will van Peer. John Benjamins Publishing Company, 1996, pp. 234–38.

Wagner-Egelhaaf, Martina, editor. *Handbook of Autobiography/Autofiction*. De Gruyter, 2017.

Walker, Barbara. "Autobiographical Practices in Russia/ Autobiographische Praktiken in Russland (review)." *Kritika: Explorations in Russian and Eurasian History*, vol. 7, no. 2, 2006, pp. 351–57.

Chapter Seven

Conclusion

LIFE WRITING AND MEMORY STUDIES

One of the most promising areas of future research is the convergence of life writing and memory studies. It is vital for us to question how people build their identities and what ideologies lie behind them. Perhaps we might look into the role of memory in life writing through the lens of cultural memory studies, where issues like resistance, ethnicity, caste and gender require more attention. Remembrance is, in fact, a political statement, and 'forgetting is the catastrophe; and a given semiotic order is obliterated' (Lachmann 302). Modes of literature such as life writing are a mnemonic art because 'writing is both an act of memory and a new interpretation, by which every new text is etched into memory space' (301).

Memory and recollection are intricately interwoven, and we live in an 'era of commemoration', as memory theorist Pierre Nora calls it. Bringing key historical events to life through literary and non-literary narratives contributes to the reframing of social memory and the formation of collective identity. Every act of commemoration makes a political statement. Indeed, our society is witnessing the passage of mnemonic narratives, which occasionally collide in the memory space. As a result, many narratives may reflect a continuous framing, unframing and reframing of public memory. Remember that memory happens only after an event, therefore, how it is framed through narratives is critical. Because of an abundance of Holocaust-related studies, the West experienced a 'memory boom' in the 1970s. There has been an explosion of edited volumes, journals and university courses on the subject because memory studies has been a promising area of research, with the culture of trauma becoming a crucial component of it.

MAURICE HALBWACHS

Maurice Halbwachs, the French sociologist, is a pivotal figure among memory studies theorists. Personal memory, in his opinion, is collective memory, since individual memory is structured by social systems. Indeed, all individual remembering occurs through the interaction of social resources, social settings, and social identities. He also discusses intergenerational memory and the social contexts in which it exists. *On Collective Memory* (1992) and *The Collective Memory* (1980) are two of the thinker's seminal works. Additionally, Halbwachs established the crucial notion of 'collective memory'. To him, collective memory is constructed and shared by a group of people.

THE QUESTION OF HUMAN RIGHTS

The social impact of life narratives on the articulation of human rights is now a major point of interrogation in the realm of Life Writing Studies. Mapping the intersections between storytelling and human rights offers exciting possibilities. Ever since 1990, after the end of the Cold War, it has turned out to be 'the decade of human rights' (Schaffer and Smith 1) as well as 'the decade of life narratives' (1). In fact, the different forms of life writing have been articulating 'a diversity of values, experiences, and ways of imagining a just social world and of responding to injustice, inequality, and human suffering' (1). Smith and Watson introduce the 'I-witness' as well as the 'eye-witness' (618), and argue that 'I' the narrator represents not only an individual but an entire group, so that the testimonial narratives depict the story of a community. They also make an interesting comment regarding the question of authenticity, or 'metrics of authenticity' (618) as they call it and conclude that 'ethical reading practices need not be based primarily on verifying claims of authenticity' (618).

Human rights life writings touching on violations such as genocide, civil war, communal riots, state oppression, etc., are 'essential to affect recourse, mobilize action, forge communities of interest, and enable social change' (Schaffer and Smith 3). In fact, these 'acts of remembering test the values that nations profess to live by against the actual experiences and perceptions of the storyteller as witness' (3). They issue an ethical call to listeners both within and beyond national borders to recognise 'the disjunction between the values espoused by the community and the actual practices that occur' (3). Such writings strongly appeal to human conscience and are capable of reframing public opinion on the occurrences described, challenging the official, statist versions of the same. Documenting the dehumanised subjectivities that gape open the wounds and the re-enactments of such excruciating experiences through writing and telling has a therapeutic effect on the victimised, in addition to having an affective impact on the readers. Life writings do offer immense possibilities for the marginalised and subalterns to communicate with readers across continents and appeal for social legislation. Such texts' narratives of 'pain, shame, distress, anguish, humiliation, anger, rage, fear, and terror, can promote healing and solidarity among disaffected groups and provide avenues for empathy across circuits of difference…' (6). The role of digital forms of life writing, such as blogs, social networking sites, in reaching more people beyond borders may also be considered very significant in the era of information technology. However, life stories depicting human rights violations are not only personal simply because of the fact that they happened in specific social contexts; we may also get to know about their wider social dimension and how they impacted the community in general. Hence, one can find a plea for community bonding in such narratives. Schaffer and Smith observe in this context: 'As balancing acts, directed back to a past that must be shared and toward a future that must be built collectively, acts of personal narrating can become projects of community building, organisational tools, and calls to action' (8). Cultural memories connected with certain incidents are invoked in the present context and are subjected to trial by the authors, and this could be capable of a transformation in the social mindset.

The different forms of life writing such as autobiographies, biographies, memoirs, diaries, etc., evoke empathy because they drive home the issue of human rights violations. In fact, this has been a major function of life narratives in the present context of atrocities. Sufferings experienced by certain sections of people are inscribed in the public sphere, appealing to readers. Obviously, there is a dominant tone of dissent and protest in these narratives. The Holocaust is a potent site of such narratives, and we have multiple memoirs that speak of untold atrocities to the entire world. When it comes to the Indian context, the Partition and the notorious Emergency caused the proliferation of many human rights discourses. The narration of first-hand witnesses have a profound impact on the readers; such writings help the subjects to unburden their 'unspeakable experiences' and we may admit here that writing has a therapeutic function. On the other hand, the ones who read these gory descriptions feel empathetic towards the subjects, and hence reading too becomes a therapy, a form of catharsis as far as readers are concerned. However, before generalising the invocation of empathy for readers, we must keep in mind the multilayered identities of readers as well as their contextual differences. It changes from one cultural context to another.

Recently, graphic novels as a mode of life writing have been effectively used by many authors, and we have graphic memoirs or autobiographical comics that represent certain painful episodes in history. Marjani Satrapi's *Persepolis* illustrates the dark episodes of Iranian history, whereas the most recent one, *Vanni* (2019) by Benjamin Dix depicts the bloody civil war of Sri Lanka. The Bhimayana series in India narrates caste discrimination in India, and works such as *Drawing the Line* (2015), are powerful visual narratives based on gender violence in the aftermath of the gruesome Delhi rape incident. Prison writing is another form that sensitises readers to human rights violations. Such narratives also come under the rubric of 'resistance narratives'.

As a form of life writing, memoir is a crucial in narrating human rights atrocities, and we have Holocaust memoirs by authors like Primo Levi's *If this is a Man* (1947), Elie Wiesel's *Night* (1960), Ann Kirschner's *Sala's Gift* (2006), Ivan Backer's *My Train to* Freedom (2016), Ariana Neumann's *When Time Stopped* (2020) and Helen Fremont's *The Escape Artist* (2020), etc., as good examples.

VANNI: A FAMILY'S STRUGGLE DURING THE SRI LANKAN CONFLICT

Vanni: A Family's Struggle During the Sri Lankan Conflict (2019) is an ethnographic graphic novel written by Benjamin Dix and illustrated by Lindsay Pollock that depicts human suffering during the Sri Lankan conflict from 2004 to 2009. The life story compassionately depicts specific real people who suffered great suffering and humiliation throughout the struggle, where two opposing perspectives of Sri Lankan politics and the relationship between the Tamil community and the Liberation Tigers of Tamil Eeelam may be seen (LTTE). Based on interviews and official documents from the civil war, the book accurately depicts the plight of Tamil refugees in Sri Lanka's northeast, and that of Tamil refugees in general.

Testimonials are also powerful platforms of self-enunciation, and Rigoberta Mechu's *I, Rigoberta Mechu* (1983) corroborates this. Television talk shows and interviews offer increased visibility to victims to share their experiences, but sometimes, if things are not handled sensitively, they stoop to such a level that the audience turn out to be voyeurs. Thus, the boundaries between private and public may get transgressed. Many authors have recently explored the potential of graphic novels as a medium for promoting human rights. As mentioned earlier, Satrapi's *Persepolis* is a very good text which narrates the trauma connected with the Iranian revolution.

Bana Alabed and Nujeen Mustafa from Syria, Yeonmi Park from North Korea and Nadia Murad from Iraq have all succeeded in using social media platforms such as Instagram, Twitter and YouTube to highlight human rights violations they have experienced. In current world, such constructions of the 'activist self' have redefined the scope of life writing. We can see how online life narratives have given these subjects/authors more visibility and made it easier for them to connect with their audiences, resulting in empathy and, as a result, an affective dimension to life writing, mediated by technology.

Stories narrating human rights violations can be emotionally charged texts, and we have perfect examples such as *I, Rigoberta Menchu*. As a matter of fact, 'storytelling has become a potent and yet highly problematic form of cultural production, critical to the international order of human rights and movements on behalf of social change' (Schaffer and Smith 31). Testimonies and subaltern life histories evoke a sense of humiliation and protest. We have good examples like Dalit life narratives and other texts by the marginalised, such as orphans, prostitutes, gays, lesbians, tribals, etc. Such life-texts provided emotional outlets in response to human rights violations and served as counter-stories to oppressive systems. On the whole, human rights life narratives bring out the tone of protest and dissent against all kinds of power structures, from a victim's perspective. Readers are also beseeched to side with the authors through their empathy. So, we can say that these works are essentially protest stories that call for fairness and justice.

DIASPORA AND LIFE WRITING

Diasporic life narratives are problematic in the sense that they are difficult to locate within 'textual boundaries' (Chansky 207), as diasporic lives shuttle between 'real and imagined spaces' (207), particularly in the context of relentless border crossings in the twenty-first century. There is a sense of instability regarding national identity in the context of a diasporic dilemma due to affiliation toward homeland or host-land. According to Leigh Gilmore, a diasporic life writer occupies an 'in-between status', a 'third space' (Bhabha and Gilmore qtd. in Chansky 211), where 'the self is always figuratively dying and being reborn in some ways as the self is continually shifting between identifying with home-nation and new nation' (211). Therefore, we need to adopt different methodologies to study diasporic auto/biographies as they construct selves which exist in multiple 'geographies, cultures, customs, and fluctuating ideas of what constitute national identities, gender constructions, and personhood' (212).

ECOLOGY AND LIFE WRITING

Alfred Hornung makes the insightful observation that life writing and ecocriticism both share a concern for the natural world and the possibility of human survival (Douglas and Barnwell 236), and that both 'represent human endeavours that seek to mediate between the fundamental elements of nature and the changing conditions of culture over time' (236). Some well-known accounts of people's lives are heavily didactic in character and have an activist agenda woven into the background somewhere. The best illustration of this can be found in *Walden* (1854), the great work by Henry David Thoreau. In fact, such narratives offer a critique of the concept of human development by drawing attention to the imminent global catastrophe and the deterioration of the environment. Many other people who write about life, such as the Harvard myrmecologist E. O. Wilson, the Japanese-Canadian biologist David Suzuki, and the ecofeminist scholar Terry Tempest Williams, have expressed their concerns regarding ecocide. A variety of literary forms, including journals, letters, memoirs, autobiographies and even television shows, have been used to depict humankind's compassionate and awe-inspiring interactions with the natural world. Viewers all over the world have gained a greater understanding of the importance of protecting the environment as a result of television networks such as *National Geographic* and *Animal Planet*.

ETHNICITY AND LIFE WRITING

With the added importance and popularity of subaltern writings across the world, ethnic life narratives are promoted by top-notch publishers, given the wider readership they are receiving. How do we approach ethnic auto/biographies in a fresh light in the context of 'ethical turn' in the humanities, bringing up the possibility of placing them within the realm of memory studies? One can notice that life writings by different groups construct collective identities, and they may thus be considered autoethnographies. Hence, reading such narratives within the framework of cultural memory studies will be a rewarding endeavour.

There are some useful tropes for approaching ethnic life narratives. Firstly, authorship is a tricky aspect because 'I' in ethnic life narratives is multiple and collective, forming a collective identity. That is why they are mostly considered autoethnographies.

For instance, in C. K. Janu's *Mother Forest*, she categorically states that 'I' is *nammal* ('us'). Quite a number of life stories by indigenous people are as-told-to narratives where one can find interlocutors narrating on behalf of the subjects, but one cannot downplay the identity politics ingrained in them. Secondly, one needs to address the politics of translation of ethnic life texts, as many are translated from regional languages. The subjects are appropriated, hijacked and even commodified by big publishing houses, keeping profit and market in mind. Third, the language of narration is important because language represents power, and many ethnic life writings deliberately break the rules and regulations of the so-called standard, mainstream language, thereby decolonising the colonial tongue. For example, Janu's autobiography narrates tribal experience in prose sans upper case or commas, signifying that dualities are insignificant. Part I of the text represents the inner world of the adivasis, by recreating the rhythm and flavour of tribal life, whereas Part II, where 'civil society' is mentioned, sticks to the formalities of language. Land is a major concern in tribal life, and violence can be seen in such life narratives where displacement occurs in the name of 'development'. Lastly, ethnic life writings interrogate the question of nation space; locating ethnic groups in the official national imaginary is problematic as they construct an oppositional, subnational space, a site of blatant discrimination. In short, it may be observed that ethnic life writings in general rehistoricise the past and inscribe a sort of 'counter-ethics' from the position of the other, reframing our set ethical notions. Through this process, human rights issues are highlighted and inscribed.

CELEBRITY LIFE WRITING

In recent years, there has been a rise in interest in Life Writing Studies and how they overlap with celebrity studies. This is based on certain common debating points such as authenticity, identity politics, ethics, etc. In fact, studies on genres such as TV documentaries, biopics, interviews, authorised biographies, and so on, are possible in these cross-disciplinary fields. If life writing and celebrity studies are dependent on discursive formations embedded in cultural practices, then celebrity culture is still centred around fame, which auto/biography studies have already deconstructed by inviting the voices of the subalterns to inscribe their lives. However, it is worth quoting Mayer and Novak here:

> Even a brief survey of life-writing scholarship and celebrity research yields a considerable pool of shared, repeatedly invoked buzzwords that point towards the two fields' many common concerns with notions of authenticity and intimacy; public and private selves; myth-making and revelation; cultural memory and identity politics. Both disciplines shine a light on the ambivalent emotional currents underlying the cultural fascination with both life narratives and celebrity, ranging from an ardent desire for emulation and hero-worship to a vengeful hunger for a socially levelling and humanizing 'dethroning.' (2)

In fact, life writing is still more inclined towards 'the seductive pull of the famous, myth-encrusted individual' (Mayer and Novak 3), purely because of the market, and we can see different versions of a subject's life because of the ideological appropriation involved.

LIFE WRITING AND AFTERLIVES

The various forms of life writing provide afterlives for the subjects they are written about. Writing records memories related to the subjects in the public domain in the form of auto/biographies, diaries, memoirs, and so on. They do, however, pass judgement on the protagonists' actions. There are certain genres, such as obituaries, that provide afterlives for deceased subjects by stressing the obit figures' heroic deeds and accomplishments. On the other hand, there are material forms such as monuments, memorials and even performative rituals that surround select figures and remind the audience of the illustrious achievements of the so-called greats who have left their own legacy. Gandhi is the ideal example, as he continues to live among us and guide our actions and thoughts. However, such life narrative variations serve as a cultural apparatus for the state. We can see how particular subjects, usually the ones with cultural capital, are appropriated and inscribed in narratives/

discourses to indoctrinate the masses. The issue of ethics may be brought up here. Life is captured and taken as a commodity in the form of a book, which is then disseminated among readers. It is indeed difficult to know what should be stated and what should be left unsaid, and the lines between them are hazy. When chosen lives, despite the politics of selection, are transferred into the textual body, the wounds inflicted on such bodies during the process of writing and, later, reading, make ethics even more perplexing.

Textual and material manifestations of the emplotment of lives through various life narratives contribute to the framing and reframing of collective memory by transforming into powerful and effective cultural apparatuses of state. People's floral tributes at major personalities' memorials and anniversary celebrations of key figures give them a new lease of life, and the former enjoy a 'continued existence' in public memory. All such public displays are held in high regard and serve as important cultural markers. Technology, both in its early stages in the form of photography and now in the format of digital space, has provided a plethora of opportunities for cultural inscription. Another fascinating aspect of these resurrected icons is their pedagogical role; short biographies or other life histories aid in the preaching of moral principles to young people who are trained to emulate their heroes. As a result, we study Harishchandra, Ashoka, Gandhi and Swami Vivekananda, to name a few. We are uninvolved with their constant presence among us; they continue to influence our thoughts and actions even after their deaths. Death, on the other hand, has granted them immortality and enhanced their power and influence.

MEDIATED LIVES: WHOSE VOICES?

As-told-to-life writing is now common, and here, the authors give agency to their subjects by documenting the latter's lives. According to Lindemann, such a form is 'the written account of a subject's life produced by a writer, on the basis of an oral account produced by the subject over the course of a series of interviews' (1). We may also call them 'spoken lives', though there is no general consensus regarding the terminology. They are also called 'as-told-to autobiography', 'the autobiography of those who do not write' (Lejeune qtd. in Lindemann 1), 'dictated autobiography' (Sanders qtd. in Lindemann 1) or 'as-told-to life narrative' (Boardman qtd. in Lindemann 1). The subjects selected for writing are abducted by the authors (Denzin 6) and their ideological leanings determine the selection and omission of incidents to be narrated. The development of technology in the form of tape recorders, cameras, portable cassette recorders and now digital technology has proved to be very beneficial to life historians in collecting data in the form of interviews and other means pertaining to their subjects. Sometimes there is a lot of excitement and hype around such narratives, arousing sensationalism and controversy as a marketing strategy. However, it may be admitted that many of these writings do not necessarily attain literary standards.

The thriving publishing industry targets saleable subjects, and people are identified to write on behalf of these subjects. Apart from a short period of publicity, many such life stories do not have lasting appeal. As-told-to life writing can be located in 'the interstices between autobiography and biography' (Lindemann 2). The subjects of such life writings appear to be vulnerable as they are not empowered enough to tell their stories with freedom and without external interference. The categorisation of this type of narrative is an issue because it is unclear if we can call it an autobiography or even a biography. Lindemann observes that 'as-told-to life writing may likewise be written in the first, second, or third person' (4) and she quotes Couser's model here:

> On one hand, there is solo autobiography, in which the writer, the narrator, and the subject (or protagonist) of the narrative are all the same person; at least they share the same name. On the other side is biography ... in which the writer and narrator are one person while the subject is someone else. In between, combining features of the adjacent forms—and thus challenging the commonsense distinction between them—is as-told-to autobiography, in which the writer is one person but the narrator and subject are someone else. (Lindemann 34–35)

However, where to place the narrator in the narrative space and what to do with the narrator's identity remain unresolved issues. Lejeune identifies two extreme types of as-told-to life writing: ghostwriting and ethnobiography. 'Ghostwriting refers to situations in which powerful subjects, usually celebrities or politicians, pay professional writers to write their life stories for them' (qtd. in Lindemann 7) and ethnobiography '...usually initiated and produced by academics or journalists and features the life stories of unknown people thought to be representative of a particular historical period, social group or community, or to be inspirational in some way' (qtd. in Lindemann 7). In the case of the first category, subjects are supremely powerful, whereas in the latter case, the authors are privileged. As-told-to life writing passes through five different stages – in 'the interview stage', writers collect data from subjects through various sittings; during 'the writing stage', they sit down to pen the details which they garnered through interviews or recordings; in 'the dialogue stage', they show the proof to subjects for feedback; during the 'publication stage' the writer and the subject ink an agreement regarding cover, finances, etc., and finally, 'the post-publication stage' where the subjects feel lost because 'the story has been told, but the life is not yet over, can be disorientating and even depressing' (Lindemann 11). The subject feels worried about his life-text because of gaps and silences in narration due to the influence of one ideology or another.

RESEARCH IN LIFE WRITING

Research in Life Writing Studies is now more interdisciplinary in nature, and with the emergence of 'hybrid and experimental forms of life writing' (Douglas and Barnwell 2), such as Instagram, vlogs and podcasts, disciplinary boundaries have become porous. Archival research is now increasingly popular in the realm of Life Writing Studies. As we know, 'archives and libraries are powerful power/ knowledge institutions and like other organisations impose strict time/space restrictions and regulations' (Tamboukou 20). The researcher who gets involved in this approach has to find, read and transcribe archival documents (20), which are characterised by narrative discontinuities (23). For instance, Couser wrote *Letter to My Father: A Memoir* by exploring his family archives. Recent autobiographical and biographical research blurs the distinction between people and objects. Igor Kopytof analyses slavery, where individuals are turned into commodities and objects, and he proposes a biographical dimension to the question of enslavement (Whitlock 35). Thus, we can see the blurring of distinction between objects and persons.

Online life writing is another bourgeoning field of research, and digital forms such as memes, You Tube videos, blogs, etc., do help in 'constructing intimate publics' (Morrison 42) through their self articulation. However, we can see that such narratives articulate new forms of 'social identity and social belonging' (46), possibly a hyperlinked subjectivity in which the authors and readers communicate directly.

Visual auto/biographical forms such as webcomics, TED talks, selfie travelogues, etc., introduce the possibility of a new digital and visual aesthetic (Brophy 53). While studying such new narratives, we may have to rethink the issues of power, agency and ethics. Compositional interpretation of images focusing on their content, colour and spatial organisation, light, and expressive content are used as methodological tropes along with semiotics and discourse analysis (Rose 73).

The oral history approach to Life Writing Studies adopts the method of interviewing subjects and documenting their life experiences. Here, memory is an important aspect to be noted because a subject's personal experiences are recounted and they necessarily have two angles; firstly, the personal is political, and remembering the past is a deliberate, selective process that involves meaningful gaps and silences, not to mention personal memory loss. Secondly, every individual has always been connected to society and other individuals, so individual remembering is personal and, more importantly, collective. This approach thus, clearly intersects life writing and memory studies, and its interdisciplinarity is also to be highlighted along with the question of the ethics of memory.

Discourse analysis can be another useful method of researching life writing. It examines the implications of power in statements, with all of their associations with caste, gender, race, ethnicity, and so on. It is essentially a study of language, both written and spoken (Griffin 93). It would be interesting to apply this method to studying autoethnographies where 'I' the subject is usually multiple and collective. An ethnographic approach helps in documenting, recording and archiving life narratives, which can be precious sources regarding certain epochs of history. It also problematises the possibility of interpreting life narratives as alternative forms of historiography. Catherine Belsey's proposed strategy of textual analysis, bringing about 'a close encounter with the work itself' (159) and its possibility in studying life narratives 'to understand the inscription of culture in its artefacts' (159) offers a new methodology in the field. Bringing Life Writing Studies and Memory Studies together gives it an interdisciplinary or even multidisciplinary dimension. In order to study the politics of autobiographical memory construction and identity formation, a memory studies approach becomes handy. Though individual memory is the chief concern, it has to be studied in a wider social context. Objectivity and truth in auto/biographical texts are usually debated and critiqued by researchers. Memory studies also play a very crucial role in analysing oral histories, as mentioned earlier. As a result, a cultural memory studies approach is extremely promising for studying various genres of life writing.

ETHICS OF LIFE WRITING

Ethics is an important question that comes up while discussing the politics of narrating lives, and critics such as Paul John Eakin consider life writing as 'a form of ethical inquiry' (243) in *The Ethics of Life Writing*. In fact, he debates about the 'harm' (1) life writing can do, apart from its potentialities in the context of lives on 'display in public' (1). As we all know, telling the truth in autobiographies and biographies, as well as crossing boundaries of privacy, are extremely sensitive issues. Those who are engaged in writing about their lives invariably make personal judgements and preach moral lessons by using their subjects as powerful cultural apparatuses.

Another aspect connected with ethics in life writing is the question of human rights. Modes of life narrative are effectively used by subaltern and other oppressed groups to articulate their painful experiences with a tone of dissent. Essentially, such narratives are pleas for human rights and the minimum human dignity of life. Eakin also hints at '...the function of life writing as a forum for the individual's claims to freedom and dignity' (5). However, a life historian has no right to hurt any subject's sentiments or make 'personal threats to the integrity of the person, such as illness and disability' (Couser 5). When there are breaches of human rights, some life narratives turn out to be 'counterstories', attacking the power structures by giving alternative versions. Writing is a political act in which certain perspectives, and thus values and morals, are fixed, and life narratives occasionally emerge debunking and delegitimising those interpretations and stories.

Finally, ethics also applies to revealing or unpacking a subject's life. Image-blasting of subjects is used in the debunking of biographies. *Eminent Victorians* by Lytton Strachey is a superb illustration of this. In this scenario, the biographer takes on the role of a burglar, breaking into the private lives of his subjects. Life narratives may also be therapeutic since the act of writing helps to unburden the subjects' painful experiences. In a nutshell, such narratives provide an ethics of care. Autopathographies or illness narratives attest to this. In some as-told-to stories, the writers, who act as mediators, hijack their subjects, and the choice of episodes to be documented is based on their ethical standpoint. There are certain instances where the genuine subjects confront their interpreters and deny their stories. It is here that the question of 'betrayal of trust' (Couser xiii) comes in, and in his significant work, *Vulnerable Subjects: Ethics and Life Writing* (2004), Couser addresses the issue of life writing and bioethics. In the representation of subjects facing certain vulnerabilities, life narrators take things for granted, breaching the boundaries of privacy and personal dignity. In fact, unwanted intrusions occur not only when writing about the lives of others by authors but also in autobiographies in which other characters are portrayed. Couser comments on this aspect in a logical manner by raising some pertinent questions: 'Are auto /biographers obliged to "do good" – or at least to do no harm – to those they represent? Can harm to minor characters in one's autobiography be dismissed as unavoidable and trivial?' (xi). However, he identifies two dimensions of such narratives: '*mimetic*, insofar as it speaks about its subject, and *political*, insofar as it speaks for its subject' (x). It may not be wise to argue for controlling and regulating life writing in connection with ethics as well.

BEYOND BOUNDARIES

Before I conclude, it is important to briefly sum up some interesting, but rather exciting, possibilities for life writing research in the present and future. With readers from all around the world, the subjects whose lives are portrayed have taken on a transnational dimension. As can be seen, it is mostly due to the effects of globalisation and cross-border migration. In this era of mobility, where the very question of identity can be problematic, the subjects are frequently involved in transit, and the fundamental notions of nation and home need to be seriously addressed. Life writing creates narrative space for the displaced and disenfranchised, allowing them to record their unique experiences for self-expression as well as political engagement. Collaborative life stories have been churned out in enormous numbers recently, and they help to form a collective identity for a group of people with loud and clear voices. Of late, archival studies are employed in auto/biography research, and critics like Tamboukou have argued that 'the materiality and sociality of the archive is crucial for the entire research process and that as researchers we should not separate the physical, social, and intellectual dimensions of the archival research we carry out' (21). One can also perceive a shift in the focus of contemporary life writing research from 'human' to 'post-human' or 'new materialisms' , where objects too are capable of evoking experiences. The so-called 'material turn' in auto/biography studies in recent decades has assisted us in reconsidering the potentialities of objects/ texts such as statues, memorials, archives, and so on. The concern for nature and its survival, the cultural locations of various subjects, and a host of other factors bring together ecological studies and life writing. The growing popularity of indigenous life narratives is another new trend in this field. Life histories of sexual minorities, (the LGBTQ community), are becoming a component of serious academic research in this domain. We may see a surge in digital lives in life writing in the coming decades of the twenty-first century, and in *Identity Technologies: Constructing the Self Online* (2014), theorists like Anna Poletti and Julie Rak have identified a link between auto/biography studies and new media studies. It is worth noting that the connection between the agent and the readers in online life narratives opens up new avenues for research. Oxford University's recent project, 'Lives in Medicine' brings together experts in the fields of clinical psychology, literature, history, etc., to identify the ways in which ailing patients recount their stories and lived experiences. An understanding of the patients' mental condition is paramount and it helps to improve the quality of treatment and medical ethics. Visual autobiographies in all their many forms, including biopics, will continue to draw a bigger audience in our society flooded with visual texts. In the case of children, various forms of life writing (for example, graphic life narratives) can be employed as pedagogical tools, and they are now seriously considered as potent modes of instruction. To conclude, the market for various forms of life writing has grown significantly, and in this already burgeoning discipline, one can witness a harmonious blending of literary inventiveness and social sensitisation.

REFERENCES

Belsey, Catherine. "Textual Analysis as a Research Method." *Research Methods for English Studies*, edited by Gabriele Griffin. Edinburgh UP, 2005.

Brophy, Sarah. "Studying Visual Autobiographies in the Post-Digital Era." *Research Methodologies for Auto/biography Studies*. Routledge, 2019.

Chansky, Ricia A. "Locating Diasporic Lives: Beyond Textual Boundaries." *Research Methodologies for Auto/biography Studies*. Routledge, 2019.

Couser, G. Thomas. *Vulnerable Subjects: Ethics and Life Writing*. Cornell UP, 2004.

---. "Making, Taking and Faking Lives: Voice and Vulnerability in Collaborative Life Writing." *Vulnerable Subjects: Ethics and Life Writing*. Cornell UP, 2004, pp. 34–55.

Denzin, Norman K. *Intrepretive Biography*. Sage Publications, 1989.

Douglas, Kate and Ashley Barnwell. "What We Do When We Do Life Writing: Methodologies for Auto/Biography Now." *Research Methodologies for Auto/biography Studies*. Routledge, 2019.

Eakin, Paul John. *The Ethics of Life Writing*. Cornell UP, 2004.

Griffin, Gabriele. *Research Methods for English Studies*. Edinburgh UP, 2005.

Lachmann, Renate. "Mnemonic and Intertexual Aspects of Literature." *Cultural Memory Studies: An International and Interdisciplinary Handbook*, edited by Astrid Erll and Ansgar Nünning. Walter de Gruyter, 2008.

Lindemann, Sandra. "As-Told-To Life Writing: a topic for scholarship." *Life Writing*, 2017, pp.1–13. doi: 10.1080/14484528.2017.1289807

Mayer, Sandra and Julia Novak, editors. *Life Writing and Celebrity*: *Exploring Intersections*. Routledge, 2020.

Morrison, Aimée. "Social, Media, Life Writing: Online Lives at Scale, Up Close, and In Context." *Research Methodologies for Auto/biography Studies*. Routledge, 2019.

Rose, Gillian. "Visual Methodologies." *Research Methods for English Studies*, edited by Gabriele Griffin. Edinburgh UP, 2005.

Schaffer, Kay and Sidonie Smith. *Human Rights and Narrated Lives*: *The Ethics of Recognition*. Palgrave Macmillan, 2004.

Smith, Sidonie and Julia Watson. *Life Writing in the Long Run: A Smith & Watson Autobiography Studies Reader*. The U of Wisconsin P, 2017.

Tamboukou, Maria. "Archival Methods in Auto/biographical Research." *Research Methodologies for Auto/biographical Research*, edited by Keith Douglas and Ashley Barnwell. Routledge, 2019.

Whitlock, Gillian. "Objects and Things." *Research Methodologies for Auto/biography Studies*. Routledge, 2019.

Glossary of Select Terms

Agency: In social science, agency refers to an individual's power to affect societal change. However, one's agency is shaped or rather constrained by factors such as religion, class and gender. In life writing, the narrative agency is critical since it plays a critical role in self-representation and identity construction.

Alterity: In philosophical and anthropological terms, alterity relates to otherness, the state of being distinct. It is a term used in media studies to refer to something unconventional and not fundamentally 'sameness'.

Anecdote: Anecdote is a term that refers to narratives about specific real-life events that are startling and engaging and eventually reflect the personality. Anecdotes are a critical narrative element that is successfully used in various genres of life writing. For example, in his biography of Samuel Johnson, James Boswell includes several tales that provide insight into his subject's unique personality.

Annals: Annals are year-by-year records of events that are historically arranged for reference.

Autoethnography: Autoethnography is a hybrid form of life narrative in which ethnographic fieldwork is used to document ethnic identity. It is a self-reflective multidisciplinary genre that spans disciplines such as history, anthropology, sociology, psychology and performance studies. Autoethnography aspires to create communal identity via the use of indigenous storytelling techniques. According to Mary Louise Pratt, autoethnography is 'colonized subjects undertake to represent themselves in ways that engage with the colonizer's own terms' (7).

Autogynography: Domna Stanton coined the term 'autogynography' in her work *The Female Autograph* (1987). It is concerned with the female autobiographical narrative and the gender issues inherent in it. In "Autogynography: Is the Subject Different?", Stanton argues that 'gendered narrative involved a different plotting and configuration of the split subject' (16) and concludes that women's autobiography is different and cannot be studied within the patriarchal framework of male autobiographies.

Autopathography: Thomas Couser coined the term 'autopathography' to describe a personal story about sickness or disability. This type, on the other hand, attempts to confront society's apathy toward patients as odd, abnormal and pathological. They may, however, be viewed as resistance narratives of survival and empowerment in the process of reclaiming the body. Thus, autopathography reveals the medical discourse's politics and the social constructions of the crippled body.

Biographee: A biography's subject is referred to as the biographee. This word was first used in 1841 and has subsequently become somewhat more prevalent. For instance, in James Boswell's *Life of Samuel Johnson* (1791), Boswell is the biographer and Samuel Johnson is the biographee.

Biography: A prominent genre of life writing, biography is the story of a person written by another person. For instance, James Boswell, the biographer, authored the biography, *Life of Samuel Johnson, LL.D.* (1791). In 1683, John Dryden coined the term 'biography'. Historical biography, psychobiography, debunking biography, hagiography and fictionalised biography are some of the branches of this form. Throughout the Middle Ages, hagiographies that exaggerated the importance of saints' lives were prevalent and were read aloud on auspicious occasions. While biography is often classified as non-fiction, fictional elements are also at times interwoven into the written account.

Biopics: Biopics are biographical films about real-life historical figures who had an impact on society. They are mostly hagiographical, drawing on personalities from domains such as politics, athletics and art, fusing reality and fiction. *Gandhi* (1982), directed by Richard Attenborough, is an excellent example of a film that weaves together pivotal moments in Gandhi's life. Numerous biopics are tainted by sensationalism and exaggeration of facts. Thus, the cinematic medium is frequently used to reinforce a particular ideology.

Blogs: Blogs or weblogs are online journals that contain words, photographs or links to personal or societal topics. Due to their interaction, blogs foster a hybridised sense of self, a rhizomatic assemblage of subjectivity. Narcissism is another major aspect of blogging. Some prominent blogging platforms are WordPress.org, Wix.com and Joomla.com. Additionally, there are vlogs, which are sites where individuals upload short videos.

Carita **or** *Carithra*: *Carita* or *Carithra* were religious biographies of Buddha written in Sanskrit or Pali. Although primarily hagiographic in nature, *carita*s were subsequently written about saints, heroes, and even military victors. Indeed, this style of character sketching straddles the line between reality and imagination. *Buddhacarita*, *Ramacarita* and *Lilacarita* are excellent representations of this indigenous genre.

Character: Character is a literary genre popularised by the ancient Greek philosopher Theophrastus, who illustrated thirty different sorts of characters in *Characters* based on virtues or vices, such as 'good man' or 'bad man'.

Chronicle: Chronicles are a methodical accounting of historical occurrences. They were immensely popular throughout the medieval period when royal families maintained chronicles. It should be noted that chronicles are devoid of commentary and analysis.

Collaborative life narrative: Collaborative life narratives are either as-told-to narratives/spoken lives in which an interviewer/writer records a subject's life experiences or, in certain circumstances, ghost-written life narratives in which an important personality's experiences are edited or structured. Occasionally, it might be a collaborative effort involving two or more people. What is crucial here is the asymmetrical power relations between the teller and the recorder; the writer's agenda generally takes precedence over the subject, and he has complete choice over which events are to be included/excluded from the text. Additionally, one can perceive an invisible power centre here, namely, a publishing firm that sets the parameters and approaches the subject as a selling commodity with the sole purpose of maximising profit. The question of agency arises here since the one with language competence and cultural capital prevails upon a subject.

Confession: Confession is an intimately personal account delivered orally or in writing to a listener or, in the ancient past, to a God who can absolve or give solutions. St. Augustine's *Confessions* reveals his spiritual progress. There are, however, other contemporary types of confessional narratives, such as talk shows, in which individuals share their struggles and triumphs. Frequently, confessions act like Pandora's box, revealing something sensational.

Diary: Diary is a daily record of significant events and transactions in a person's life. Diary writing was a popular literary pastime in the seventeenth century, particularly in France. However, this style only gained popularity with the publication of Samuel Pepys' *Diaries*. A journal is sometimes used interchangeably with a diary, as it documents the occurrences of a certain period of time. *The Journal of a Tour to the Hebrides* (1785) by James Boswell is a well-known journal.

Discourse: The word 'discourse' was popularised by the French philosopher Michel Foucault and refers to the exchange of ideas and knowledge, as well as the covert operations of power and their impact on society. It structures language and gives special weight to particular ideals and assumptions, for example, legal discourse and medical discourse.

Genealogy: Genealogical charts record a family's ancestry and are critical for researching a subject's family history in the field of life writing. They are not, however, as extensive as family history. Investigating the ancestors of royalty and aristocracy was a popular practice in historical genealogical investigations. Tracing genealogy becomes critical in the field of medical research as well.

Genre: Genres are classifications of creative or literary works based on their content, style or form. The common genres of literature are novels, poetry and drama. However, there are several sub-genres of novels, such as science fiction, detective fiction, graphic novels, historical novels and campus fiction, to name a few. It may be added that genre crossovers are widespread in contemporary writing.

Graffiti: Graffiti is a term that refers to inscriptions on walls that depict dramatic personal experiences. While the events themselves may not be organised or full, the memories frozen on walls do inscribe identities, both personal and collective. While authorship or agency may be a problem in the case of graffiti, one cannot ignore the subaltern, counter-narratives' underlying ideological implications. Another intriguing aspect is that graffiti may occasionally convey a feeling of communal identity when a message of shared dissent is conveyed.

Hagiography: Hagiography, according to Merriam Webster, is the biography of saints or venerated individuals. They are often encomiastic in character and contain details about the saints' passions, temptations and miracles.

Identity: Identity refers to an individual's uniqueness or personality, and according to Merriam Webster, it is the state of being identical to anything expressed or affirmed. Numerous genres of life writing, including autobiography and biography, investigate and textualise the intricate layers of individual subjects.

Ideology: Ideology is a set of shared views and values held dear by an individual or group. Karl Marx defined ideology as 'false consciousness' that is inextricably linked to the material circumstances of life. Louis Althusser defined ideology as the process by which distinct state apparatuses interpellate individuals as subjects.

Intention: In literary studies, intention means the aim or purpose of an author.

Interviews: Interviews are personal narratives of self-disclosure in which the interviewer unravels the subject's psyche. However, pauses and silence may occur throughout an interview, and the issue of truth is often raised.

Journal: A journal is a daily record of events, occurrences, experiences and ideas. It is distinct from a diary in that it is not as intimate or personal. A good example is *A Journal of the Plague Year* (1722) by Daniel Defoe, which is an account of a person's experiences in 1665, during the bubonic plague's rampage through London. Philip Lejeune, the noted French professor and essayist, used the terms journal and diary interchangeably.

Letters: A letter is a mode of private correspondence, with its own set of specific etiquette rules through which inner feelings are communicated. According to Sidonie Smith, 'letters become vehicles through which information is circulated, social roles enacted, and relationships secured, often in a paradoxical mix of intimacy and formality' (196). However, letters also transmit class, caste, gender, ethnic origin and national origin ideals. Though most letters remain unpublished, others, such as Jawaharlal Nehru's *Letters From a Father to His Daughter* (1929) touch on social developments as well.

Literary autobiography: They are autobiographies by accomplished authors that reveal their artistic evolution and how their minds and memories aided in the creation of their art. In this sense, William Wordsworth's *The Prelude: On the Growth of a Poet's Mind* (1850), James Joyce's *A Portrait of the Artist as a Young Man* (1914–15), Angelou's *I Know Why the Caged Bird Sings* (1969), etc., are literary autobiographies.

Memoir: Memoirs are loosely structured mnemonic narratives about the lives of others based on their own experiences. Essentially a French term, *memoire* was introduced in England in the early eighteenth century. In comparison to autobiography, memoirs are disorganised, gossipy, and tend to focus on the lives of others. However, both terms are frequently used interchangeably in current parlance. Lee Quinby observes, '[W]hereas autobiography promotes an "I" that shares with confessional discourse an assumed interiority and an ethical mandate to examine that interiority, memoirs promote an "I" that is explicitly constituted in the reports of the utterances and proceedings of others. The "I" or subjectivity produced in memoirs is externalized and . . . dialogical' (299). They are written in a variety of contexts, including domestic and secular. *Walden* by Thoreau, *Night* by Elie Wiesel and *If This Is a Man* by Primo Levi are all good examples of memoirs. Almost always, the goal of a memoir is to leave a personal legacy rather than to pursue literary excellence.

Memory: Memory is a narrative that is constructed after an event and is transferred in a variety of ways, including writing. However, tangible items such as sculptures and museums also serve to crystallise memories. Our individual and collective social identities are defined by our memories. Memory studies, as an interdisciplinary field, connects interestingly with life writing.

Narrative: Narrative is concerned with how a tale is presented, whereas life writing is engaged with the presentation of many events in a subject's life. However, the experiences included in a life story are chosen according to the author's ideological leanings in their various manifestations.

Obituaries: Obituaries are narratives that contain value judgments about well-known individuals who were popular and had an impact on society. They occur in a variety of media outlets, including newspapers, periodicals, TV channels and social media posts. An obituary may be viewed as a cultural apparatus, with the obit subject serving as a symbol for the encoding of particular collective memories.

Other: The other is a person or group of people who are regarded as inferior or marginalised based on their gender, sexual orientation, race, or caste. These less fortunate individuals endure exploitation and humiliation at the hands of the dominant group. Jacques Lacan defined the subject with the capital letter 'Other'.

Personality: It refers to the uniqueness of a character with all its mental, psychological and social dimensions.

Portrait: A portrait is a written representation of a person, a biography. However, the narrative is given less importance and the emphasis is placed on showing the personality. Lytton Strachey's *Portraits in Miniature* (1931) is an excellent example, as it contains astute observations of individuals such as James Boswell.

Prison narratives: Prison narratives are protest narratives against a system that attempts to inhibit the victim's self within degrading settings. Indeed, Barbara Harlow divides inmates into two categories – common law detainees and political detainees – but maintains that they cannot be easily distinguished (457). She adds that in the detainees, 'their personal itineraries, which have taken them through struggle, interrogation, incarceration, and, in many cases, physical torture, are attested to in their own narratives as part of a historical agenda, a collective enterprise' (455).

Profile: A profile is a concise biographical summary of a person, highlighting just the most salient characteristics.

Reminiscences: A book-length compilation of recollections and personal encounters. *Reminiscences* (1866) by Thomas Carlyle and *Reminiscences and Correspondence* (1869) by Henry Crabb Robinson are excellent examples.

Self-help narratives: Self-help narratives have a motivational and therapeutic effect on readers seeking a formula for increasing their skill levels in order to achieve success. They have an enduring impression on readers when recounted via engaging narratives about their quest for achievement in today's world of fierce competition.

Subject: The subject is the individual about whom a life narrative is written. It is employed in conjunction with the self and the individual, although post-structural theories emphasise its fractured identity.

Spiritual autobiography: Spiritual autobiography, also known as religious autobiography, is a story of one's spiritual salvation. While the majority of religious autobiographies are based on Christian tradition (such as St. Augustine's *Confessions*), religious autobiographies also exist in Judaism, Islam and other religions. Essentially, they are all stories of conversion aimed at a broader audience.

Testimonio: Testimonio is a Spanish term that means 'testimony or bearing witness or attesting something'. John Beverley defines testimonio as 'a novel or novella-length narrative in book or pamphlet . . . form, told in the first person by a narrator who is also the real protagonist or witness of the events he or she recounts, and whose unit of narration is usually a "life" or a significant life experience' (92–93). Testimonies are quite often made on behalf of a suffering community; it is witness narrative with an ideological leaning on the 'affirmation of the individual self in a collective mode' (97). Some of the most popular testimonies are John Bunyan's *Grace Abounding to the Chief of Sinners* (1666) and *I, Rigoberta Menchu* (1983).

Witnessing: Witnessing is an eyewitness account of trauma addressed to a real or imagined audience. Kelly Oliver observes, 'Witnessing has the double sense of testifying to something that you have seen with your own eyes and bearing witness to something that you cannot see' (18). A witness's exposition of excruciating experiences is first-hand knowledge that has a touch of authenticity.

Who's Who: *Who's Who* is a biographical dictionary of life sketches of prominent persons. Published at regular intervals, it is essentially a British publication and its American counterpart is *Who's Who in America*.

REFERENCES

Beverley, John. "The Margin at the Center: On 'Testimonio'." *De/Colonizing the Subject*, edited by Sidonie Smith and Julia Watson. U of Minneosota P, 1992, pp. 91–114.

Harlow, Barbara. "From a Women's Prison: Third World Women's Narratives of Prison." *Feminist Studies*, vol. 12, no. 3, 1986, pp. 501–24.

Oliver, Kelly. *Witnessing: Beyond Recognition*. U of Minneosota P, 2001.

Pratt, Mary Louise. *Imperial Eyes: Travel Writing and Transculturation*. Routledge, 1992.

Quinby, Lee. "The Subject of Memoirs: *The Woman Warrior*'s Technology of Ideographic Selfhood." *De/Colonizing the Subject*, edited by Sidonie Smith and Julia Watson. U of Minneosota P, 1992, pp. 297–320.

Smith, Sidonie and Julia Watson. *Reading Autobiography: A Guide for Interpreting Life Narratives*. U of Minneosota P, 2001.

Stanton, Domna C. "Autogynography: Is the Subject Different?" *The Female Autograph*, edited by Domna C. Stanton. New York Literary Forum, 1984, pp. 3–20.

Further Reading

Adams, Katherine. *Owning Up: Privacy, Property, and Belonging in U.S. Women's Life Writing*. Oxford UP, 2009.

Adams, Marie. *The Myth of the Untroubled Therapist: Private Life, Professional Practice*. Routledge, 2014.

Anjaneyulu, T. *The Art of Biography*. Christian Literature Society, 1982.

Arnold, David, and Stuart Blackburn, editors. *Telling Lives in India: Biography, Autobiography and Life History*. Permanent Black, 2004.

Baena, Rosalia, editor. *Transculturing Auto/Biography: Forms of Life Writing*. Routledge, 2007.

Basavaraj, S. Naikar. "The Autobiographies of Nehru and Chaudhuri - A Comparative Study." *Comparative English Literature*, edited by Manmohan K. Bhatnagar. Atlantic, 1999.

Battersby, James L. "Narrativity, Self, and Self-Representation." *Narrative*, vol. 14, 2006, pp. 27–44.

Beard, Laura J. "Indigenous Auto/Biographical Writings in the Americas." *a/b: Auto/Biography Studies*, vol. 31, no. 3, 2016.

Benson, Michael. *Cosmigraphics: Picturing Space through Time*. Abrams, 2014.

Beth, Sarah. "Hindi Dalit Autobiography: An Exploration of Identity." *Modern Asian Studies*, vol. 41, no. 3, 2007, pp. 545–74.

Bhabha, Homi K, editor. "Narrating the Nation." Introduction. *Nation and Narration*, Routledge, 1990, pp. 1–8.

Bingham, Dennis. *Whose Lives Are They Anyway? The Biopic as Contemporary Film Genre*. Rutgers UP, 2010.

Boldrini, Lucia, and Julia Novak, editors. *Experiments in Life-Writing: Intersections of Auto/Biography and Fiction*. Springer, 2017.

Bose, Sugata, and Ayesha Jalal. *Modern South Asia: History, Culture, Political Economy*. Routledge, 2003.

Bourdieu, Pierre. "The Biographical Illusion." *Identity: A Reader*, edited by Paul Du Gay et al. Sage, 2000, pp. 297–303.

Brewster, Anne. *Reading Aboriginal Women's Autobiography*. Sydney UP, 1996.

Brien, Donna Lee, and Quinn Eades. *Contemporary Life Writing Methodologies and Practice*. UWA P, 2018.

Bruss, Elizabeth. *Autobiographical Acts: The Changing Situation of a Literary Genre*. Johns Hopkins UP, 1976.

Butalia, Urvashi. "Community, State and Gender: Some Reflections on the Partition of India." *Women and the Politics of Violence*, edited by Taisha Abraham. Haranand, 2002, pp. 125–59.

---. *The Other Side of Silence: Voices from the Partition of India*. Penguin, 1998.

Callewaert, W., and R. Snell, editors. *According to Tradition: Hagiographical Writing in India*. Harrassowitz, 1994.

Cardell, Kylie. *Contemporary Uses of the Diary*. U of Wisconsin P, 2014.

Carroll, Sean. *The Big Picture: On the Origins of Life, Meaning, and the Universe Itself*. Dutton, 2016.

Chakrabarty, Dipesh. *Habitations of Modernity: Essays in the Wake of Subaltern Studies*. Permanent Black, 2002.

Chaney, Michael, editor. *Graphic Subjects: Critical Essays on Autobiography and Graphic Novels*. U of Wisconsin P, 2011.

Chatterjee, Partha. "The Nationalist Resolution of the Women's Question". *Recasting Women: Essays in Colonial History*, edited by Kumkum Sangari and Sudesh Vaid. Kali for Women, 1989, pp. 233–53.

Chellappan, K. "The Discovery of India and the Self in three autobiographies." *The Colonial and the Neo- Colonial Encounters in Commonwealth Literature*, edited by H. H. Gowda. U of Mysore, 1983, pp. 95–106.

Chute, Hillary. *Disaster Drawn: Visual Witness, Comics, and Documentary Form*. Harvard UP, 2016.

---. *Graphic Women: Life Narrative & Contemporary Comics. Gender and Culture*. Columbia UP, 2010.

Civale, Susan. *Romantic Women's Life Writing: Reputation and Afterlife.* Manchester UP, 2019.

Couser, G. Thomas. *Memoir: An Introduction.* Oxford UP, 2012.

----. "Disability and (Auto) Ethnography: Riding (and Writing) the Bus With My Sister." *Journal of Contemporary Ethnography*, vol. 34, no. 2, 2005, pp. 121–42.

---. *Signifying Bodies: Disability in Contemporary Life Writing.* U of Michigan P, 2009.

---. *Vulnerable Subjects: Ethics and Life Writing.* Cornell UP, 2004.

---. *The Work of Life Writing Essays and Lectures.* Routledge, 2021.

Delafield, Catherine. *Women's Diaries as Narrative in the Nineteenth-Century Novel.* Ashgate, 2009.

Devika, J. "Housewife, Sex worker and Reformer: Controversies of Women Writing Their Lives in Kerala". *Economic and Political Weekly*, vol. 41, no. 17, 2006, pp. 1675–83.

---. "The Aesthetic Woman: Re-forming Female Bodies and Minds in Early Twentieth Century Keralam." *Modern Asian Studies*, vol. 39, no. 2, 2005, pp. 478–79.

D'Souza, Lawrence. *Autobiography in Indian Writing in English.* Cyber Tech, 2009.

Duguay, Stefanie. "Lesbian, Gay, Bisexual, Trans, and Queer Visibility Through Selfies: Comparing Platform Mediators Across Ruby Rose's Instagram and Vine Presence." *Social Media and Society*, Apr–June 2016, pp. 1–12. http:// journals.sagepub.com/doi/abs/10.1177/2056305116641975.

Eakin, Paul John. *How Our Lives Become Stories: Making Selves.* Cornell UP, 1999.

---. *Writing Life Writing: Narrative, History, Autobiography.* Routledge, 2020.

---, editor. *The Ethics of Life Writing.* Cornell UP, 2004.

---. "Autobiography as Cosmogram." *Storyworlds*, vol. 6, 2014, pp. 21–43.

Edel, Leon. *Literary Biography.* Rupert Hart Davis, 1957.

El-Rafaie, Elizabeth. *Autobiographical Comics: Life Writing in Pictures.* UP of Mississippi, 2012.

Fawcett, Fred. *Nayars of Malabar.* Government P, 1901.

Felman, Shoshana, and Dori Laub. *Testimony: Crises of Witnessing in Literature, Psychoanalysis, and History*. Routledge, 1992.

Franklin, Cynthia G. *Academic Lives: Memoir, Cultural Theory, and the University Today*. U of Georgia P, 2009.

Fuchs, Miriam, and Craig Howes, editors. *Teaching Life Writing Texts, Options for Teaching*. Modern Language Association, 2007

Gilmore, Leigh. *The Limits of Autobiography: Trauma and Testimony*. Cornell UP, 2001.

Herges, Katja and Elisabeth Krimmer, editors. *Contested Selves: Life Writing and German Culture*. Camden House, 2021.

Hirsch, Marianne. *The Generation of Postmemory: Writing and Visual Culture After the Holocaust*. Columbia UP, 2012.

Hoskins, Janet. "Agency, Biography and Objects." *Handbook of Material Culture*, edited by Christopher Tilley et al. Sage, 2006.

Jeffrey, Robin. *The Decline of Nair Dominance: Society and Politics in Travancore, 1847-1908*. Manohar, 1994.

Kumar, Uday. "Autobiography as a Way of Writing History: Personal Narratives from Kerala and the Inhabitation of Modernity." *History in the Vernacular*, edited by Raziudhin Aquil and Partha Chatterjee. Oxford UP, 2004, pp. 418–48.

---,"Consciousness, Agency and Humiliation. Reflections on Dalit Life Writing and Subalternity." *The Political Philosophies of Antonio Gramsci and B. R. Ambedkar*, edited by Cosimo Zone. Routledge, 2013, pp. 158–70.

---. Dr. Palpu's Petition Writings and Kerala's Pasts. Nehru Memorial Museum and Library, 2014. NMML Occasional Papers, *History and Society*, 59.

---. "Self, Body and Inner Sense: Some Observations on Sree Narayana Guru and Kumaran Asan." *Studies in History*, vol. 13, no. 2, 1997, pp. 247–70.

Kunka, Andrew J. *Autobiographical Comics. Bloomsbury Comics Studies*. Bloomsbury, 2017.

Lejeune, Philippe. "The Autobiographical Pact." *On Autobiography*, edited by Paul John Eakin. Translated by Katherine Leary. U of Minnesota P, 1989. pp. 3–30.

---. *On Diary*, edited by Jeremy D. Popkin and Julie Rak. Translated by Katherine Durnin. U of Hawai'i P, 2009.

Maguire, Emma. *Girls, Autobiography, Media: Gender and Self-Mediation in Digital Economies*. Palgrave Macmillan, 2018.

Majeed, Javed. *Autobiography, Travel, and Post-National Identity: Gandhi, Nehru and Iqbal*. Palgrave Macmillan, 2007.

Marcus, Laura. *Auto/Biographical Discourses: Theory, Criticism, Practice*. Manchester UP, 1994.

Martínez García, Ana Belén. *New Forms of Self Narration: Young Women, Life Writing and Human Rights*. Palgrave Macmillan, 2020.

McNeill, Laurie, and Kate Douglas. "Teaching Lives: Contemporary Pedagogies of Life Narratives." *a/b: Auto/Biography Studies*, vol. 32, no. 1, 2017.

McNeill, Laurie, and John David Zuern. "Online Lives 2.0: Introduction." *Biography*, vol. 38, no. 2, 2015, pp. v–xlvi.

Menchú, Rigoberta. *I, Rigoberta Menchú: An Indian Woman in Guatemala*. 1983, edited by Elisabeth Burgos-Debray. Translated by Ann Wright. Verso, 1984.

Morrison, Aimée. "Facebook and Coaxed Affordances." *Identity Technologies: Representing the Self Online*, edited by Anna Poletti and Julie Rak. U of Wisconsin P, pp. 112–31.

Nakamura, Lisa. "Cyberrace." *Identity Technologies: Constructing the Self Online*, edited by Anna Poletti and Julie Rak. U of Wisconsin P, 2014, pp. 42–54.

Nandy, Ashis. *Intimate Enemy: Loss and Recovery of Self under Colonialism*. Oxford UP, 1986.

Nayar, Pramod K. "Autobiogenography: Genomes and Life Writing." *a/b: Auto/ Biography Studies*, vol. 31, no. 3, 2016, pp. 509–25.

Oliver, Kelly. *Witnessing. Beyond Recognition*. U of Minnesota P, 2001.

Olney, James, editor. *Autobiography: Essays Theoretical and Critical*. Princeton UP, 1980.

Pascual Soler, Nieves. *Food and Masculinity in Contemporary Autobiographies*. Palgrave Macmillan, 2018.

Personal Narratives Group. *Interpreting Women's Lives: Feminist Theory and Personal Narratives*. Indiana UP, 1989.

Poletti, Anna. *Stories of the Self: Life Writing after the Book*. New York UP, 2020.

Poletti, Anna, and Julie Rak. "Introduction: Digital Dialogues." *Identity Technologies: Constructing the Self Online*, edited by Anna Poletti and Julie Rak. U of Wisconsin P, 2014, pp. 3–22.

Popkin, Jeremy D. "Life Writing in the Family." *a/b: Auto/Biography Studies*, vol. 25, no. 2, 2010, pp. 172–85. Taylor & Frances Online, doi:10.1353/ abs.2010.0038.

Rak, Julie, and Anna Poletti, editors. *Identity Technologies: Constructing the Self Online*. U of Wisconsin P, 2014.

Ramaswamy, Vijaya, and Yogesh Sharma. *Biography as History: Indian Perspectives*. Orient Blackswan, 2009.

Saksena, S. P., editor. *Indian Autobiographies*. Oxford UP, 1949.

Schafer, Kay, and Sidonie Smith. *Human Rights and Narrated Lives*. Palgrave Macmillan, 2004.

Smith, Sidonie, and Julia Watson. *Reading Autobiography: A Guide to Reading Life Narratives*. U of Minnesota P, 2010.

---. "Virtually Me: A Toolbox about Online Self-Presentation." *Identity Technologies: Constructing the Self Online*, edited by Anna Poletti and Julie Rak. U of Wisconsin P, 2014, pp.70–95.

Stanley, Liz. "The Epistolarium: On Theorizing Letters and Correspondences." *Auto/Biography*, vol. 12, 2004, pp. 201–35.

Stephenson, Jenn. *Performing Autobiography: Contemporary Canadian Drama*. U of Toronto P, 2013.

Summerfield, Penny. *Histories of the Self: Personal Narratives and Historical Practice*. Routledge, 2019.

Tamboukou, Maria, and Mona Livholts. *Discourse and Narrative Methods*. Sage, 2015.

Thumim, Nancy. *Self-Representation and Digital Culture*. Palgrave Macmillan, 2012.

White, Hayden. "The Value of Narrativity in the Representation of Reality." *Critical Inquiry*, vol. 7, 1980, pp. 5–27.

Whitlock, Gillian, and Anna Poletti. "Self-Regarding Art." *Biography*, vol. 31, no. 1, Winter 2008, pp. v–xxiii.

Winstead, Karen A. *Oxford History of Life Writing, Vol 1 The Middle Ages*. Oxford UP, 2018.

Wood, Mary Elene. *Life Writing and Schizophrenia*. Rodopi, 2013.

Zuern, John. "Online Lives: Introduction." *Biography*, vol. 26, no. 1, 2003, pp. v–xxv.